AN INTRODUCTION
TO TRANSFORMATIONAL
GRAMMARS

An
Introduction
to
Transformational
Grammars

EMMON BACH

The University of Texas

Holt, Rinehart and Winston, Inc.

NEW YORK, CHICAGO, SAN FRANCISCO

COPYRIGHT © 1964 BY HOLT, RINEHART AND WINSTON, INC.
ALL RIGHTS RESERVED
LIBRARY OF CONGRESS CATALOG CARD NUMBER: 64-12732

20747-0114

PRINTED IN THE UNITED STATES OF AMERICA

234362
X
P 201 . B2 .

c

PREFACE

Since the publication of Noam Chomsky's *Syntactic Structures* in 1957 there has been a steadily growing interest in the approach to linguistic theory and description known as transformational grammar. This interest has been evidenced by the reissue of that book, by the increasing number of transformational studies appearing in the published literature, and by the addition of courses on transformational grammar to linguistics programs at various institutes and universities. At the same time there has been a lack of a simple step-by-step presentation of the concepts, techniques, and problems of that theory. This book, which has grown out of a course given by the author at The University of Texas, has been written to fill that need.

Transformational theory is still in a stage of rapid growth. Hence this introduction cannot present securely established results only; it also guides the reader to various problems and questions that are still very much under discussion. The complaint has been voiced that workers in this field have used obscure and undefined terminology. Actually, this is not the case, but a good deal of the basic literature is buried in fairly technical discussion — often difficult to obtain — or masked in polemics. It is hoped that this book will help communication by gathering into one place a discussion of some of the basic notions and techniques of the theory.

The emphasis is less on the theoretical side of the subject than on the practical problems of language description. In line with this aim, a number of problems have been included. They are intended to furnish the reader with materials for becoming acquainted with the basic considerations and manipulations of a grammar of rules. It has been my experience that the more theoretical discussions acquire meaning only after one has had some practice in using the "language" of transformational grammars for describing linguistic structures. No attempt has been made to give an adequate sampling of the different types of structures encountered in various languages. The problems can be easily supplemented by other sets of data, or the deeper study of one language can be undertaken in conjunction with a study of the book. In general, there is no one "right" answer for most of the problems. If the book is used by a class, much can be learned by comparing different solutions as to their intrinsic merits and by considering the implications of the various possible solutions in the context of a more complete set of rules.

Basically, I have written for a reader who is conversant with most of the techniques and terms of modern descriptive linguistics. On the other hand, I have assumed nothing in the way of a background in mathematics or symbolic logic.

In the interests of clarity, it might have seemed preferable to postpone the discussions of remaining issues and alternatives to the end of the book. However, it seemed more natural to discuss some of these problems in the main body of the text. A few sections that are not too essential to a first reading have been starred. They may be glossed over in a first reading and returned to later. It must be emphasized from the outset that many of these issues are peculiar to transformational theory only to the extent that it attempts to be more explicit than many other approaches.

In general, I have not argued extensively the advantages of transformational theory over other schools of linguistics. It is hoped that the book may contribute in some small way to the advent of a time when it is no longer necessary to qualify the name of our science by such adjectives as "structural," "American," or "modern."

It is a pleasure to acknowledge my indebtedness to various students, friends, and colleagues both at The University of Texas and elsewhere. In particular I extend thanks to Robert P. Stockwell for the opportunity to attend his seminar on transformational analysis at the 1961 Linguistic Institute at The University of Texas, to Robert T. Harms for many hours of fruitful discussion, to William F. Klatte, Wayne Tosh, W. P. Lehmann, Larry Martin, and especially to Noam Chomsky, Paul M. Postal, and Leonard Newmark for comments and suggestions on this book. I am also grateful to the following persons for supplying or checking examples: Robert Hugh Meskill, Ralph D. Anderson, Mrs. Elli Marlow, and Joseph L. Conrad. Finally, I wish to thank Jean Raub Bach for constant encouragement and editorial comment and Mrs. Anna Wirth Thompson for a difficult typing job well done. The necessary time to complete most of the writing of this book was made possible through the Linguistic Research Center of The University of Texas and the National Science Foundation.

E. B.

Austin, Texas
January 1964

CONTENTS

AN INTRODUCTION
TO TRANSFORMATIONAL
GRAMMARS

CHAPTER ONE

INTRODUCTION

1.1 The Task of Linguistics

The Greek philosopher Aristotle divided human intellectual activities into three kinds: practical, artistic, and theoretical. When we concern ourselves consciously with language at all, this concern is usually of a practical sort, directed at learning or teaching a language, deciding what turn of phrase to use in an important letter, urging a school board to adopt or not to adopt the teaching of languages in elementary schools. Occasionally we consider language in the sphere of art, when we read, interpret, or perhaps create a poem or a novel. These are works that embody in the medium of language the esthetic values of the individual or the community.

Linguistics, however, is not concerned with language from either of these viewpoints. Rather, it is concerned with the theoretical study of language, the result of the urge to understand, explain, and predict the facts of language: people talking to each other or to themselves, understanding or misunderstanding what they say; people using their particular inheritance from the tower of Babel to pray, argue, or make love; to write letters or poems, advertisements, or critiques of pure reason. The product of this study is a theory — a theory about a particular language and a theory about language in general.

Linguistic theories are sets of statements about language. Linguistics must make use of a language itself to form these statements. One purpose of this book is to present a kind of language about language. Most of the readers of this book will have had the experience of learning a second language. To a certain extent, the problems encountered in learning a new natural language will be duplicated here. To learn Greek or Menomini or Korean it is not enough to read through a compact presentation of paradigms or rules. It is essential to gain practice in repeating sentences and forming new ones; in short, to use the language as much as possible. Likewise here. Numerous examples and problems are presented throughout this introduction. They should be worked through carefully. The success of the reader will depend on the extent to which he exploits this illustrative material (or even supplements it). Discussions of the theoretical issues raised by transformational theory will have little meaning until the basic concepts and symbols have been mastered.

However, if transformational theory consisted merely of a new set of symbols and conventions for presenting well-known facts, there would be little point in learning the conventions. And indeed, we shall consider various specific claims about the types of structures encountered in natural languages and the grammatical theories needed to account for them. General linguistic theory (insofar as it is concerned with the formal side of language) must present a set of terms and distinctions sufficient to account for the rich variety of grammatical systems given in the world's several thousand languages, but limited enough to explain the universal features of these natural languages. Each theory of a specific language can then be taken as a particular exemplification of the types of systems predicted by general linguistic theory. To the extent that the notions of transformational theory are adequate to this task, it offers a preliminary picture of what languages in general are like.

1.2 The Data of Linguistics

The major emphasis of this book lies on the terms and devices that can be used for constructing grammars. The concepts of the theory are presented gradually so that a full picture of the system emerges only after the first few chapters. Here, we shall consider briefly the facts of language that we must take as given, that is, as empirical data that need to be accounted for by any adequate theory.

First of all, there is a physical and physiological side to language. It is often said that the linguist begins by segmenting the stream of speech into discrete units of sound. Such a statement embodies a misleading metaphor. An act of speech is a series of disturbances in a conducting medium, a series of muscular and neural changes. Once the act is performed, it is gone forever. We can no more segment it than we can segment a sunrise. What we can do is record the event with varying degrees of approximation to an ideally complete (and hence impossible) replication. The record can be of two kinds. It might be a series of X-ray photographs, a tape-recording, a spectrogram. Or, rather than a physical record like the foregoing, it might be a symbolic *representation* of the event. In either case it is only the record of the speech act that can be segmented and manipulated. What is usually meant by the metaphor is something like this: the first task of the linguist is to choose a set of symbols for representing the stream of speech.

It is a commonplace to say that a "complete" record of an utterance is of little interest for linguistic science, or is at most only the first step toward a more adequate representation. Even where the interest of the linguist is focused on the sounds of speech, it is not the sounds as acoustic or physiological events that are of interest but rather the "significant" features of these sounds. Language is a social institution. For this reason the data of linguistics are not mere physical events, but physical events together with judgments of the native speaker about these events.

In other words, in linguistics "empirical" is not to be equated with "physical." What we must account for includes what is known as the native speaker's "intuition" about what he says and hears, what the Germans call *Sprachgefühl*. The term "intuition" is a loaded and ambiguous word; therefore, it will be avoided wherever possible in this exposition. Nevertheless, the fact remains that language as a cultural product cannot be adequately studied apart from the native speaker's judgments. These judgments are of several kinds.

The native speaker judges some utterances as being repetitions of the "same" sentence, phrase, or word. No two utterances are ever exactly alike. But in any speech community some utterances will "count as" repetitions, while others will not. And it is only the native speaker's judgment that can tell us about this fact. The attempt to account for this cultural datum has occupied the energies of linguists over the last few decades and has led to a theory of representation called phonemics.

Because phonology (to choose a more neutral term) is closely related to the physical side of speech, it is easy to fall into the error of imagining that phonology is somehow more "objective" or sure than the other parts of linguistic study. It must be made plain, however, that the entities postulated by the phonologist are completely hypothetical constructs. A phonemic theory about a language is just that: a theory which can be shown to be wrong, but which can never be proved. A scientific theory is a provisionally accepted set of hypotheses.

Next, the native speaker judges only some utterances to be genuine utterances of his language. This process of accepting some sets of noises and rejecting others need not be conceived of in a literal way. Only in rather artificial situations (such as linguistics or language classes) will the speaker make statements like "Yes, you can say that," "No, it isn't 'gooder,' it's 'better'," and so on. But certain utterances will be passed over and understood with no special comment, whereas others will provoke raised eyebrows, laughter, or puzzlement. For instance, if on the first day of the semester I begin my lecture by saying: "Therefore, we must conclude that a language is an infinite set of sentences," the members of the class will probably begin to look at each other, ask what day it is, and so on. If I continue by saying, "For to complicated otherwise assumes to all sorts of unled foundations," the reaction will be stronger. If I then look at the class and say, "Am what is bothering you is that I talking incoherent English?" the atmosphere will become very uncomfortable. Further, speakers of a language constantly make mistakes and correct themselves. Recently a public speaker said: "His was a life cut soon too short"; he pondered a moment and then changed it to "cut short too soon."

Here again, a linguistic theory must account for the fact that certain sequences are "in" the language and others are not. In this connection one must insist that the theory account primarily for the "ordinary" sequences that need no special interpretation or far-fetched contexts. For example, suppose two men are setting up the solid letters on a theater marquee. One of them might say, "The 'of' looks rather fragile." In this context the sentence is perfectly understandable. Yet a theory of English which put the form *of* in the same class as *jug*, *glass*, *statue*, and *girl* would be completely chaotic.

The minimal requirement that we can place on a theory about a particular language is that it specify or predict all and only the sentences of the language. Both "all" and "only" are necessary. The following "grammar" will specify all the sentences of written English: "Take one or more marks of punctuation and one or more words from Webster's English Dictionary and string them together." The instruction will account for any English sentence. In fact, it will account for any sequence of English sentences such as the works of Shakespeare or the entire contents of the *Encyclopaedia Britannica* (with certain obvious exceptions). On the other hand, the following "grammar" will specify only sentences of written English: "The following sequences are English sentences: *John likes fish, Molly lives in the Coral Gables Apartments, Othello was a jealous Moor.*" It is only when we take the two requirements together that we can speak seriously of a grammatical theory. The first grammar will not only specify all the sentences of English but many other sequences as well such as *a aa A acid,,: aam Aani aar aardvark.* The second grammar (even if extended to include all the sentences of the *Encyclopaedia Britannica*) will not predict all possible English sentences (it would be safe to bet that it would not include a perfectly ordinary sentence like *He sold me a goat*) and certainly tells us nothing about how English works. The fact that no such theory for any language has yet been devised is of no significance. The "all and only" statement is almost a tautology, rather like the statement "An adequate physical theory must account for all physical events (and no theological ones, and so on)."

In order to meet (or approach) this minimal requirement, it is apparent that we must state just how our theory about a particular language does specify or predict the sentences of the language. Rather than state this separately for each particular theory, we make this description of the sentence-specifying capacity of grammatical theories a part of general linguistic theory.

However, an empirically adequate theory of a natural language must do more than merely specify the well-formed sentences of a language. There are many other facts about the sentences of a language that must be explained by a linguistic theory. Some sentences have the same structure even though they are composed of totally different forms. Some sentences are understood in a certain way parallel to other sentences of a different structure. Some sentences are related in a definite way to certain other sentences. Some sentences are ambiguous, and so on. In order to account for these data (which are as surely part of the proper concern of linguistics as are the judgments about phonemic "sameness" or sentencehood), we insist that a grammatical theory not only specify just the sentences of the language but also tell us in a determinate way the structure of the specified sentences. Or, as we shall say, the grammar must assign a "structural description" to each sentence.

A few examples will make this point clear. The following two sentences have the same structure at an appropriate level of abstraction. Our theory of English sentence structure must embody this fact.

Some birds eat worms.

The man who was walking down the street looked at the girl leaning out of the third-floor window of the Wrigley Building.

Or consider the relation between *essay* and *translate* in

The essay was difficult to translate.

Now you have to translate the essay.

It is clearly the same, while a single relationship (different from the preceding one) holds between the words *student* and *translate* in

The student was anxious to translate.

The student has to translate the essay.

Our theory of English must not only show that these are all perfectly ordinary sentences of English (and not, for instance, *The essay was anxious to translate* or *The student was difficult to translate*) but must provide an explicit basis for explaining the native speaker's understanding of the relationship between the sentences. Similarly, it must show the difference between the two overtly parallel sentences:

The candy is to eat.

The boy is to play.

Again, consider these sentences

1. His swimming was a mistake.
2. His swimming was mediocre.
3. His swimming was fantastic.
4. For him to swim was a mistake.
5. His having swum was a mistake.

Here we must account for the fact that the phrase "his swimming" is understood in different ways in (1) and (2); that (3) can be understood in two ways; that the way in which (1) is understood is closely related to the way in which (4) and (5) are understood; and that *His having swum was fantastic* is no longer ambiguous.

(All of this must be accounted for, and, in addition, the fact that
we do not say *For him to swim was mediocre*, and so forth.)

Again, a theory of English must show that all of these sentences
are well-formed

> I wanted to go.
> John wanted to go.
> I wanted John to go.
> John wanted me to go.

and that *I wanted me to go* is not. Further, it must explain the fact
that *John wants John to go* is about two different people called
"John."

Finally, there exist special relationships between certain pairs of
sentences. Thus we say that *The fish was eaten by a pelican* is the
passive of *A pelican ate the fish*. *What is he?* corresponds as a
question to the answer (say) *He is a farmer* and not to *He is
Captain John Smith*. Further, if the answer is given *He is the
farmer*, we understand this in a special way, for example, 'He's the
one taking the part of the farmer in the play,' or the like.

In the following chapter we shall begin the study of systems of
linguistic description which specify the well-formed sentences of a
language. In subsequent chapters we shall extend the discussion to
systems which not only carry out such specification but also assign
structural descriptions to the specified sentences. From both
standpoints we shall find statements called transformations to be
necessary. That is, transformations are needed in order to build
efficient sentence-specifying theories and also to provide the
structural descriptions that will account for many facts like those
illustrated above. Our attention will be directed mainly toward the
parts of language known traditionally as morphology and syntax.
In Chapter 6, however, we shall consider briefly some questions
that arise in accounting for the phonological facts of a language
within a transformational theory.

CHAPTER TWO

SOME BASIC NOTIONS

2.1 Grammars and Languages

Like most words in our language, the word "grammar" is used in several different senses. It may mean a particular kind of book, a textbook for learning a language, or a reference book for looking up various points of usage. It may mean the system of a language, the underlying regularities obeyed by speakers of the language. Or it may mean a series of statements or formulas describing this underlying structure, in short, a theory about the language. We shall use the term in this last sense.

The particular way of stating a theory of a language with which we shall be concerned has taken its inspiration from modern logic. In the last century a great deal has been learned about the structure of deductive systems (systems of logic, mathematics, axiom systems for various sciences). Logicians and mathematicians have been concerned more and more with studying various "language systems" or "calculi" from an abstract point of view. At the same time, modern linguistics has tended toward describing languages as abstract and formalized systems. In many ways the theory of language presented here may be considered the result of a convergence between these two currents. The grammars that we shall study are attempts to state the principles by which sentences of a language may be constructed, in much the same way that a formalized mathematical theory may be used to construct theorems.

We require that the theory be **formal, explicit,** and as **complete** and **simple** as possible. These are, of course, requirements for an ideal theory; any actual grammar will fail to a greater or less degree in one or another point.

A theory of a language is called **formal** if it refers to the actual signs (letters, phonemes, words, and so on) of the language and not to their meaning. It should be borne in mind that this requirement, like the others, refers to the theory itself and not to a particular presentation of it in a book. Thus, a statement that "verbs denoting desire" require an object in a certain case is not a formal statement. It might very well be appended to a theory as an explanation to the reader but could not itself form part of the theory. To qualify as part of a formal theory it would have to be translated into formal terms: for instance, a series of steps allowing the production of the actual combinations of forms by means of lists and rules. Nor does the requirement of formality refer to the analytical operations carried out in order to arrive at the theory.

By **explicitness** is meant the requirement that the theory itself state the relationships between the forms, that by a series of "mechanical" steps the forms of the language may be produced in proper sequence and combination with a minimum of interpretation left to the intelligence of the reader or user of the theory. Just what this minimum is — that is, what is meant by "mechanical" — will become clear below (see also Section 2.5).

At this point it is well to recall the obvious distinctions with which we began. A pedagogical grammar will depend a great deal on the linguistic intuition of the user as well as on the existence of certain universal, or near universal, properties of languages. It will generally be aimed at a user who is a speaker of a particular language and will exploit this fact in choice and emphasis. But a theory of a language can do no such thing, or else there would be many theories of the same language (one for native English speakers, one for Thai speakers, and so on). Further, we cannot compare two theories as to simplicity if one is more explicit than the other.

The most important reason for insisting on the two closely related requirements of formality and explicitness is, however, the following. The statements of a scientific theory must be testable; that is, it must be possible to match them up against some empirical observation and decide whether they are true or false. Now consider some such statement as this: "The relative pronoun (in such and such a language) must agree with its antecedent in gender and number." How are we to test such a statement? The rule is clear enough to someone who already knows a good deal about the language; thus it is an appropriate part of, say, a pedagogical grammar. But it is formulated in highly abstract terms. It is only after we have specified in detail the answers to questions like "What is a relative pronoun?" "Under what conditions can we say that a given form is the antecedent of a relative pronoun?" and so on, that the statement becomes testable. The grammars we shall study are attempts to provide such detailed specification.

There will be more to say about the requirements of completeness and simplicity later. Suffice it to say here that a complete theory will cover all the facts of the language. When two theories cover the same facts, the one that does this with a shorter set of statements is the simpler. In other words, the simpler theory will have more general statements and fewer special ones. It is important to bear in mind that simplicity must be considered in relation to the whole theory. If statements about only a part of a language, say its sound system, can be simplified but only at the expense of greater complication elsewhere in the theory, this consequence must be considered when deciding whether or not to incorporate the partial simplification.

In discussions of the sort we shall be undertaking here, the term "language" is often used in a very abstract and general sense. For our purposes, a language is a set (class) of objects constructed out of a set of elements by stringing them together through an operation called **concatenation** (literally, 'chaining together'). The objects so constructed — including the case of a single element — are called **strings**. In actual systems of language this operation may be thought of as specifying an order in time, or an order from left to right, from top to bottom, outward and clockwise, and so on, in various possible writing systems. Thus, one possible string constructed out of the elements *Bill, piano, plays,* and *the* is *Bill plays the piano.* The elements may be anything whatsoever. For example, signals of green, yellow, and red lights may be taken as the elements of the language of traffic lights. Very often we shall use simple artificial languages utilizing only a few elements such as *a, b,* and so on, for problems and illustrations of general principles.

More precisely, we must say that a language is a subset (subclass) within the set of all possible strings of the elements in question. Most languages with which we are familiar permit only a part of all possible strings. For instance, in English we cannot say *Piano the plays Bill.* Or we may imagine a language with two elements *a* and *b,* in which only strings of the form *ab, abab, ababab,* ··· are permitted, but none of the forms *aa, aba, baba,* ···. The permitted strings are called the well-formed or grammatical **sentences** of the language. Of course, since any set (according to the conventions of set theory or the algebra of classes) is a subset of itself, a system in which any sequence whatsoever were permitted would still fall within the bounds of this definition.

Natural languages — Thai, Japanese, Mr. Hyman Kaplan's brand of English — have certain characteristics among the class of languages in our general sense. First of all, not all sequences of the elements (phonemes, phones, morphemes, phrases) are permitted. Hence, a theory about some natural language cannot be simply a list of the elements; the theory must somehow show how these elements are combined into sentences.

Second, although every sentence is finite in length, there is no upper limit to the length of permitted sequences. For example, the longest English statement ever made can be extended by prefixing to it *I know that* ···, *I know that I know that* ···, and so on. Or consider the sentence *There are two guinea pigs in the field.* The form *two* can be replaced by any number whatsoever and the result will still be an English sentence. It follows that the number of different sentences is infinite. This is an important fact. From it we must conclude that our description of any language cannot be simply a list of the permitted sequences — no matter how arranged — for surely our theory must be finite in length. The study of the ways in which languages manage to provide an infinite number and variety of sentences (by means of processes more interesting than the ones illustrated above) has been one of the most fruitful directions of research initiated by transformational theory.

This point has often led to misunderstandings and resistance. It is probably true that no English sentence longer than a million words has ever been uttered. It is safe to predict that none ever will be. If, however, we set some arbitrary upper limit to the length of sentences (and hence make the language described by the grammar a finite set of sentences), this will merely complicate our task enormously. The point is that there are certain basic processes in the structure of the language that can be reapplied indefinitely many times. The fact that there are limits to these processes can then be attributed to certain practical limitations of the users of the language.

What the further distinguishing characteristics of natural languages may be is a question to be answered by a general theory of language. We are far from being able to answer it in any detail, but an important insight has been gained in recent research in the realization that part of the answer to this question can come only from a formal and abstract study of languages and grammars.

A (**generative**) grammar of a language is a theory or set of statements which tells us in a formal and explicit way which strings of the basic elements of the language are permitted. (A somewhat more adequate version of this statement will be developed in the next few chapters, where we shall in addition require that the grammar tell us about the structure of each permitted string.)

2.2   Standard Form for Grammatical Theories

To ensure a maximum uniformity in formality and explicitness (so
that two grammars may be compared and one chosen as the better
theory), it is necessary to state our grammatical theories in a
standard form.

A **grammar** shall consist of a set of symbols interrelated by an
ordered set of rules. Every **rule** is of the form

$$X \rightarrow Y$$

and may be interpreted as an instruction to rewrite X as Y. Among
the symbols of the grammar (its "vocabulary") there are some
which never appear to the left of the arrow in a rule as symbols
to be replaced. These are called **terminal symbols** (with respect to
the set of rules). Among the nonterminal symbols there is at least
one **initial string** of symbols which is taken as given by the theory
(in the fashion of a primitive term in a chain of definitions or an
axiom in a deductive theory).

The symbol for concatenation is usually a plus sign $+$ (sometimes an arch $\cap$ or an ampersand $\&$). Where there is no danger
of confusion, we shall often suppress the concatenation sign.

The symbols $\rightarrow$, $+$, $(\ )$, $\{\ \}$, $[\ ]$ are defined in the metatheory, the general theory about theories about languages (the
various types of brackets are discussed below, 2.3). The other
symbols — the representations for forms, classes, constructions and
so on, for example, S (sentence), NP (noun phrase), and so on —
are set up for the purposes of describing particular languages. The
eventual aim of general linguistic theory is to have these latter
symbols defined, at least in part, by the metatheory also. To the
extent that symbols defined by a general phonetic theory are used
in the phonetic representations of the grammar, this is indeed
the case.

Among the elements assumed to be available for each grammar
(or component of a grammar) there is one which plays a special
role, namely, the **null** (**unit** or **identity**) element. It functions in
the mathematical system underlying the representations of a

grammatical theory as does zero in ordinary addition, or the digit 1 in ordinary multiplication: *null* + *x* = *x* + *null* = *x*. That is, when the null element is concatenated with any string, that string remains unchanged. This element must be sharply distinguished from a "zero-morph" or the like, which is an element functioning like any other overt symbol in the grammar, but which is replaced by null at some point or level in the grammar.

A grammar for a given language, then, will take the form described above and will be constructed in such a way that the terminal strings (the strings consisting wholly of terminal symbols) will directly represent sentences of the language. The specification (or generation) of the terminal strings of the grammar is carried out by applying the rules first to an initial string, then to every subsequent string to produce a derivation. A **derivation** (of a given string from a given grammar) is a sequence of strings of symbols of which the first string is an initial string and in which every string **follows from** the preceding one by the application of a rule. That is, the strings XYZ and XWZ can be succeeding lines in a derivation if and only if there is a rule $Y \rightarrow W$ (or a rule $XYZ \rightarrow XWZ$). In passing from one line of a derivation to the next, one and only one rule may be applied.

Here is an example of a simple grammar:

Initial string: Z

RULE 1. $Z \rightarrow A + B$
RULE 2. $A \rightarrow C + D$
RULE 3. $C \rightarrow c$
RULE 4. $D \rightarrow d$
RULE 5. $B \rightarrow b$

From this grammar we can produce by the following derivation one and only one terminal string:

Z	(given)
$A + B$	(RULE 1)
$C + D + B$	(RULE 2)

$c + D + B$ (RULE 3)
$c + d + B$ (RULE 4)
$c + d + b$ (RULE 5)

In this example the capital letters are the nonterminal symbols, the lower-case letters are the terminal symbols.

We saw above that natural languages are infinite sets of sentences. A grammar of the form illustrated will, however, generate only a finite number of terminal strings (no matter how long and detailed). In order to provide for an infinitude of terminal strings, a grammar must have a basic property called **recursiveness**. Suppose we add to our grammar a new optional rule

3a. $D \rightarrow Z$

and allow the strings to run through the rules again as long as they still contain nonterminal symbols. Now our grammar will generate an infinite set of terminal strings, all of the form *cdb*, *ccdbb*, *cccdbbb* $\cdots$. An element like Z in this example is called a **recursive** element because strings can be derived from it that contain the same element. We shall consider in the following chapters the important question of just where and how this necessary recursive property can best be built into a grammar.

Suppose we wish to allow a replacement for a given nonterminal symbol in certain contexts only; for example, Y may be rewritten as W only if it immediately follows Z. This can be done either by a rule

$Z + Y \rightarrow Z + W$

or as follows:

$Y \rightarrow W$ in the environment $Z + -$.

Here — shows the place in the string where the given replacement is to be permitted. Sometimes we write "in env." for short or simply "in." Such a rule is called a **context-sensitive** or **context-restricted** rule.

In giving the form of a grammatical rule above $(X \rightarrow Y)$, nothing was said as to the types of structures represented by X and Y. In the grammar above the items to the left and right of the "rewrite" arrow are strings of symbols. It is according to the restrictions on the scope of X and Y that different types of grammars and different components in a single grammar are distinguished. We shall take up three main types of rules: phrase-structure (Chapter 3), transformational (Chapter 4), and phonological (or morphophonemic) rules (Chapter 6).

2.3   Abbreviative Notations

Often a number of alternative rules may apply to a given symbol. In such cases several abbreviative devices may be used to collapse several rules into a single one.

For the two rules

$A \rightarrow B$
$A \rightarrow B + C$
(but not $A \rightarrow C$)

we write

$A \rightarrow B(C)$

That is to say, ordinary parentheses are used to enclose optionally chosen items.

For the two rules

$A \rightarrow B$
$A \rightarrow C$

we may write

$$A \rightarrow \begin{Bmatrix} B \\ C \end{Bmatrix} \quad \text{or} \quad A \rightarrow \{B, C\}$$

That is, alternative replacements for a symbol (which must not both be chosen at a single application) are listed vertically within braces (not parentheses) or horizontally within braces and separated by commas. The latter notation is useful as a space-saving device where long lists, as of lexical items, are given. Where there is no danger of confusion the braces are often omitted around a horizontal listing.

Finally, for the rules

$$A + B \rightarrow D + B$$
$$C + B \rightarrow E + B$$
$$\text{(but not } A + B \rightarrow E + B)$$

we may write

$$\begin{bmatrix} A \\ C \end{bmatrix} B \rightarrow \begin{bmatrix} D \\ E \end{bmatrix} B$$

Occasionally, it is useful in complicated rules to number the brackets which correspond on both sides of the arrow. The square brackets tell us that if we have the first element in the (first) pair of brackets on the left, then we must replace it by the first element in the (first) pair of brackets on the right, similarly for the second item, and so on.

These types of abbreviated rules can be put together into various combinations. Thus the rule

$$X \begin{bmatrix} A \\ B \end{bmatrix} \rightarrow X \begin{bmatrix} a \begin{Bmatrix} b \\ c \end{Bmatrix} (d) \\ \left\{ (e) \begin{Bmatrix} f \\ g \end{Bmatrix} \right\} \\ h \left(\begin{Bmatrix} i \\ j(k) \end{Bmatrix} \right) \end{bmatrix}$$

is an abbreviation for twelve rules. I shall refer to rules which contain no parentheses, braces, or brackets as **minimal** rules. (Some writers use numbered pairs of braces in the way that the square brackets are used here.) The braces and brackets can also be used in giving environments.

Besides providing a more compact notation which leads us to seek more general formulas, these devices offer a further advantage. If we have a series of minimal rules giving alternative replacements for a single item, we must specify that the choices are all optional except for the last (which must apply if none of the previous changes have been made). By using such devices as the parentheses and braces, we can build the options directly into the rule, so that all rules of this type must be applied wherever the items to the left appear in a string but may be applied in differing ways.

The function of the concatenation symbol is to set apart and define the minimal symbols of the grammar. Since this separation is already accomplished by the various kinds of brackets and braces in our abbreviated rules, it is not necessary (indeed, it is misleading) to include a plus sign between a symbol and a bracket (brace, and so forth). The concatenation sign may be automatically written into derivations between any two symbols separated in a rule by such a mark.

2.4   Some Examples

The symbolism introduced above offers a compact and uniform way to state many of the relationships described by traditional and modern grammars: immediate constituency, class membership, complementary distribution and so on, as in the following examples:

A sentence consists of a subject and predicate.

Sentence → Subject + Predicate

Man, boy, girl, chair are nouns.

$$Noun \rightarrow \begin{Bmatrix} man \\ boy \\ girl \\ chair \end{Bmatrix}$$

The plural morpheme Z_1 is represented by the allomorph /s/ after /p t k/, and so on.

$$\begin{bmatrix} p \\ t \\ k \\ etc. \end{bmatrix} Z_1 \rightarrow \begin{bmatrix} p \\ t \\ k \\ etc. \end{bmatrix} s$$

In other words, in a generative grammar names for classes, constructions, and so on, can become explicitly functioning elements in the system of the rules.

In order to become accustomed to this symbolism, let us consider two extended examples, first of all, a phonemic system (system of basic sounds and their possible combinations) for a hypothetical language. I shall state the facts for the language in ordinary English and then give two descriptions, the first in a form familiar to students of modern linguistics, the second as a set of "rewrite" rules.

Language X has the following phonemes: three consonants /p k l/, three vowels /i a u/, one stress phoneme /'/. Every form consists of one or more syllables. Every syllable consists of a nucleus, an optional initial string of consonants, and an optional final consonant. The nucleus consists of one or two vowels. The initial consonants may be /p/ or /k/ with or without a following /l/. The final consonant must be /l/. Stress may occur (distinctively) on the first vowel of any syllable. All combinations of vowel plus vowel occur as nuclei except /ii/. Since certain sequences of vowels are distinct according to how they are arranged into syllables, we set up in addition to the phonemes listed above a phoneme of syllable boundary /-/ (the presence of which is predictable in terms of the surrounding phonemes in many sequences). The phonemes have the following conditioned variants (allophones): /p k/ are voiced between vowels, /a/ is [ə] except where stressed. The consonant /p/ is aspirated immediately before a stressed nucleus (with or without an intervening /l/).

DESCRIPTION 1. We may summarize the phonotactics of Language X by the following formulas:

$$F = S(-S)(-S) \cdots \qquad \text{(\textit{F: form; S: syllable})}$$

$$S = \left(\begin{Bmatrix} p \\ k \end{Bmatrix} (l) \right) \overset{(')}{V^1}(V^2)(l) \qquad \begin{array}{l} \text{(\textit{V}}^1\text{: }/i\ a\ u/;\ V^2\text{: }/a\ u/\ \textit{where}\\ V^1\ \textit{is }/i/,\ /i\ a\ u/\ \textit{elsewhere)} \end{array}$$

We may summarize the allophonic system thus:

Phoneme	has the allophone	in the environment
/p/	[b]	$V — V$
	[pʿ]	$—(1)\acute{V}$
	[p]	elsewhere
/k/	[g]	$V — V$
	[k]	elsewhere
/l/	[l]	everywhere
/a/	[a]	´
	[ə]	elsewhere
/i/	[i]	everywhere
/u/	[u]	everywhere
/'/	[']	everywhere

DESCRIPTION 2. This system may be described by a set of rules as follows:

Initial string: F

1. $F \rightarrow S(-F)$

2. $S \rightarrow \left(\begin{Bmatrix} p \\ k \end{Bmatrix} (1) \right) (')\, V(V)(1)$

3. $p(1)' \rightarrow p'(1)'*$

4. $V - \begin{bmatrix} p \\ k \end{bmatrix} V \rightarrow V - \begin{bmatrix} b \\ g \end{bmatrix} V$

5. $VV \rightarrow \begin{Bmatrix} ə \\ u \\ i \end{Bmatrix} V$

6. $iV \rightarrow i \begin{Bmatrix} ə \\ u \end{Bmatrix}$

---

* In such rules we follow the convention that a parenthesized element on both sides of the arrow remains unaffected. The rule is thus short for

$pl' \rightarrow p'l'$ and $p' \rightarrow p''$.

Since we have so far considered only arrangements of symbols in a linear sequence, the stress mark is here written as preceding the stressed vowel rather than above it.

7. $V \rightarrow \begin{Bmatrix} \text{ə} \\ \text{u} \\ \text{i} \end{Bmatrix}$

8. $'\text{ə} \rightarrow '\text{a}$

There are several important differences between these two descriptions. Description 2 is considerably shorter than Description 1. That is, if we count all the occurrences of the symbols denoting sounds or classes of sounds (omitting symbols of the metalanguage, that is, parentheses, arrows, and so on) which are used for the essential parts of the two statements, the second one uses fewer symbols. This characteristic will be discussed later as a possible formal measure of simplicity. Description 2 is considerably more unified. That is, where the first description has marginal definitions (for example, of V^1 and V^2), in the second description such general symbols as S, V, and so on, are defined by the rules and form an integral part of the rules. The second description is more explicit and has fewer loose ends. For example, compare the use of the symbol V in the two treatments. Or compare the two counterparts to the statement "Every form consists of one or more syllables." In the first description ($F = S(-S)(-S) \cdots$) it is left entirely to the reader to interpret this formula. The second description accomplishes the same result (an indefinite number of syllables strung together) by a process of recursive derivation:

F
$S - F$
$S - S - F$
$S - S - S - F$

The derivation can be continued as long as desired and cut off at any point simply by not taking the optional F to the right of the arrow.

Most important at this point, perhaps, is the general character of Description 2. A string of symbols is run through an ordered set of rules somewhat like an assembly line in a factory. At each step the string is scanned to see whether it contains the symbols specified to the left of the arrow. If it does, the operation of replacement is carried out and the derivation with its new final line is sent on to the next rule. It is the ordered character of the rules which makes it unnecessary to include the "elsewhere" statements of Description 1 and which leads us to choose the more general allophonic symbol "ə" for the phoneme /a/ from the outset. The reader may object that this choice could be made in Description 1 as well. The point is, however, that there is no particular reason in Description 1 for doing so.

It should be noted that there is no stage at which the strings of Description 2 appear in a purely phonemic transcription. As the reader can convince himself, a restatement of the rules in which there is a clean break between phonotactic and allophonic rules will require a longer description. Rule 4 illustrates a situation of the sort which has led to the use of a distinctive feature phonology in transformational grammars (see Section 6.3).

On the whole, order of statements is more crucial in the second description. In Description 1 the specification of allophones for each phoneme is given in a certain order, that is, the special statements before the "elsewhere" statements. On the other hand, there is no particular reason for listing the phonemes in the order given. In the second description, however, some rearrangements would necessitate many changes in the rules, and in some instances would make the rules unworkable. If Rule 4, for instance, did not precede the development of V in Rules 5, 6, and 7, it would have to take some such form as this:

$$
\begin{bmatrix} ə \\ u \\ i \end{bmatrix} - \begin{bmatrix} p \\ k \end{bmatrix} \begin{bmatrix} ə \\ u \\ i \end{bmatrix} \rightarrow \begin{bmatrix} ə \\ u \\ i \end{bmatrix} - \begin{bmatrix} b \\ g \end{bmatrix} \begin{bmatrix} ə \\ u \\ i \end{bmatrix}
$$
$$
1 \ 1 \qquad 2 \ 2 \quad 3 \ 3 \qquad 1 \ 1 \qquad 2 \ 2 \quad 3 \ 3
$$

All of these rules are of a type that we shall call **string-replacement** rules in contrast to complex rules of a transformational sort. That is, they apply to strings of elements according to their shape alone at a given point of the derivation. A rule like 7 applies to the actual symbol V (in this instance, all the V's that have not been covered by the preceding two rules). The rules do not consider earlier parts of a derivation showing where an element comes from.

For a second extended example let us consider English noun inflection. The main features can be handled by rules of the following sort:

Given: *Noun*

1. $Noun \rightarrow \begin{Bmatrix} Noun_m \\ Noun_p + Z_1 \\ Noun_c(Z_1) \end{Bmatrix} (Z_2)$

2. $Noun_m \rightarrow$ milk, bə́tir, rays, piys, fədž, bləd

3. $Noun_p \rightarrow$ ǽnil, mı́yzil, ayd, pı́ypil, səspéndir, pænt, sı́zir

4. $Noun_c \rightarrow$ mæn, wúmən, aks, wayF, boy, stik, piys, ridž, natš, fináminən, hen, šiyp, tšayld, læf, pæΘ, hawS, deΘ

5. $\begin{bmatrix} \text{pı́ypil} \\ \text{šiyp} \\ \text{mæn} \\ \text{wúmən} \\ \text{aks} \\ \text{fináminən} \\ \text{tšayld} \end{bmatrix} Z_1 \rightarrow \begin{bmatrix} \text{pı́ypil} \\ \text{šiyp} \\ \text{men} \\ \text{wímin} \\ \text{áksin} \\ \text{fináminə} \\ \text{tšı́ldrin} \end{bmatrix}$

6. $\begin{bmatrix} F \\ \Theta \\ S \end{bmatrix} Z_1 \rightarrow \begin{bmatrix} v \\ đ \\ z \end{bmatrix} Z_1$

7. $Z_1 + Z_2 \rightarrow Z$

8. $\begin{Bmatrix} Z_1 \\ Z_2 \end{Bmatrix} \rightarrow Z$

9. $\begin{bmatrix} F \\ \Theta \\ S \end{bmatrix} \rightarrow \begin{bmatrix} f \\ \theta \\ s \end{bmatrix}$

10. $Z \rightarrow$ iz in env. $\begin{Bmatrix} s \\ z \\ š \\ ž \end{Bmatrix} —$

11. $Z \rightarrow s$ in env. $\begin{Bmatrix} p \\ t \\ k \\ f \\ \theta \end{Bmatrix}$ —

12. $Z \rightarrow z$

In considering such examples of limited problems, it must be remembered that their solution may be quite different if more of the total context of a grammar is taken into account (in line with our requirement that simplicity be measured ideally in terms of a complete theory).

In the first rule, English nouns are broken down into three subclasses according to their co-occurrence with the plural morpheme (Z_1): mass nouns $(Noun_m)$ which do not occur in the plural, plural nouns $(Noun_p)$ which do not occur in the singular, and count nouns. (We must consider such nouns as *pants* and *scissors* to contain the plural morpheme because of their verbal suffix selections: *The scissors are here.*) Any of these can occur with the possessive morpheme (Z_2). Of course, in a full grammar of English many more subclasses are necessary, and the attachment of the possessive would take place at some other point or points. Rule 1 simply summarizes the possibilities for noun inflection which arise throughout the grammar.

Rules 2, 3, and 4 supply the lexicon, that is, the lists of forms belonging to the most detailed subclasses of the grammar. Notice that it is not necessary to distinguish homonyms like *peace* $(Noun_m)$ and *piece* $(Noun_c)$ except where distinct representations must be retained for later rules. In German, for instance, we must distinguish /baŋk/$_1$ 'bank' from /baŋk/$_2$ 'bench' in order to produce the proper plural forms /báŋkən/ and /béŋkə/. The noun bases are represented morphophonemically. We distinguish the final morphophonemes in *laugh* and *wife* on the basis of their plural formation (see Rule 6). The morphophonemic symbols "F, θ, S" are, in our terms, simply nonterminal symbols of the grammar.

Such devices have long been used in morphophonemic descriptions and illustrate the close connection between transformational theory and some preceding trends in modern (and ancient Indian!) linguistics. The forms "fədž, natš," and so on, were represented in that way (rather than by means of "ǰ" and "č") to illustrate the way in which the decision to consider a whole theory may influence choice of alternatives on a lower level. The more traditional phonemic representation would force us to add two more symbols to the environments listed in Rule 10. Needless to say, this analysis might not stand up in the light of a complete phonological theory for English.

Rule 5 provides for some exceptions to the general methods of plural formation in English. Rule 6 — by means of the special symbols mentioned above — takes care, in effect, of another list of nouns (*wife, life, knife, calf, path*, and so on). Such a technique is useful whenever the listing would be prohibitively long. Any such special rules are placed before the general rules. After passing Rules 5 and 6 there will no longer be any instances of "aks + Z_1" or "wayF + Z_1" to produce the incorrect plural forms "aksiz" or "wayfs." Rule 7 collapses any instances of the two suffixes which are left at this point into a single morphophoneme "Z." Rule 8 obliterates the distinction between "Z_1" and "Z_2," which is no longer needed. (A simple addition will allow the rules to cover the verbal suffix of *stops, reaches, wins* or the forms of *is* in *Pat's coming, John's coming.*) Rule 9 accounts for the choice of allomorph to go with possessive suffix as well as for uninflected forms in the nouns with voiced-voiceless alternations in the final consonant. The last three rules produce the regular alternations of the allomorphs of the plural. The last one — which occurs in the largest variety of environments — is left as the standard, or "elsewhere," form. This arrangement appears to be the most economical one when the environments are specified by phonemes; the same ordering is apparently demanded by a distinctive feature specification (see Halle, 1961*).

---

* References throughout this book are to the works listed by author and year in the Selected Bibliography, pp. 189–193.

2.5   General Remarks

Two difficulties face the reader at the outset of his study of the kind of grammatical theory we are presenting. One is the idea that the rules of a generative grammar must be explicit, that given a few simple directions (with regard to symbols like →, ( ), and so forth) the derivation of strings could be carried out by a mechanical application of the rules. A similar reorientation in thinking is required of a person learning to write programs for an electronic computer, where an operation that is relatively simple for a human intelligence must be broken down into a large number of exceedingly simple and exasperatingly moronic steps.

At this point we can state a little more precisely what is meant by a "mechanical" application of the rules. We assume a device of some sort containing a set of rules of the form described above. The device is capable of accepting a string of concatenated symbols and of recognizing when the string (or some substring) is identical with the left-hand side of some rule. We set the device at Rule 1 and feed it a string of symbols. If Rule 1 does not apply, the device moves to Rule 2 and examines the string again (similarly for any subsequent rule). If a rule does apply (if some substring is recognized as the left member of the rule at hand), the device first copies down the examined string on an output tape, then copies down on the "examination tape" a new string which is identical with the old string but with the right member of the rule applied in place of the substring found to be identical with the left side of the rule. Before changing to the next rule, the new string is scanned again. When several rules have the same left member (alternatively, when there are abbreviated rules with braces and parentheses), the device makes some arbitrary choice. To this extent, then, the device is not wholly "deterministic" or mechanical. When the rules are exhausted, the process terminates. The content of the output tape is then the derivation of some terminal string (or nothing, if the original input matches nothing in the derivation machine). This is, of course, not the description of some actual machine but an intuitive picture of the system of description we are considering.

(This picture will be modified by later discussion, particularly that of Chapter 4.)

We do not have to look far for the reason for insisting on this detail. If we wish to understand the working of a language in all its detailed complexity, we must take care that our descriptions do not assume the very abilities that we are trying to explain. The test of a grammatical theory (not a pedagogical grammar) is not the relative ease with which a mature person can learn a language from the theory. An analogy from the field of phonetics may be helpful. Everyone knows that the best way to teach the correct pronunciation of a foreign language is by imitation and drill with a trained teacher (with perhaps a modicum of physiological explanation). Yet we cannot hope to understand the processes of phonation without a detailed examination of all the minute adjustments and interconnections of the speech organs (as undertaken, for instance, in Pike, 1943).

The other difficulty is almost the opposite one, namely, accepting the idea that there is no mechanical way of operating on the data (at least by any presently known methods) to arrive at the "right" set of rules. It is necessary to step back from a preoccupation with the shape of the actual bits of language (what will be directly represented by the terminal strings) and to use the full range of possibilities in setting up all kinds of nonterminal elements, arranged perhaps in quite a different order from the actual order of sentences. Many of the basic terms of modern linguistics have been described in terms of operations on "raw" data. Transformational theory takes a radically different viewpoint. The difference becomes clear when we compare two attempts to define a grammatical category such as "Adjective" for a given language. One statement for English reads: "Any word having the distributional characteristics of *slow* and capable of being modified by the addition of *-er* and *-est* is an adjective, and the resultant constructions containing the postbases *-er* and *-est* are also adjectives" (Hill, 1958, page 168). In a generative grammar, on the other hand, any item will "be" an adjective in a given derivation if it is derived from the symbol

Adjective by the application of a chain of rules beginning with a rule of the form

$$Adjective \rightarrow X$$

That is, it will be ultimately a listing (perhaps recursive) which defines the members of the class *Adjective*. These two "definitions" are not as far apart as some would argue. Rather, they are different ways of looking at the same facts. In the second instance, the fact that adjectives may be compared by the addition of *-er* and *-est*, that adjectives of the same subclass as *slow* will appear in the same contexts (distribution) as *slow*, and so on, will result automatically from the rules. We shall follow here the point of view that it is futile to search for a definition of items outside the theoretical structure of the grammar, that the grammar itself offers an extended definition of the items postulated, and that the ultimate justification of the items set up and defined by the grammar is nothing but the adequacy and simplicity of the total theory. An important contribution of transformational theory has been the realization that linguistic "structure" is always relative not just to the data or corpus but also to the grammatical theory describing the data, and that the way in which a theory assigns a structural description to the sentences it generates must be spelled out in detail.

Problems for Chapter 2

All of the following problems involve rules which are string-replacement rules (Section 1.4) but otherwise unrestricted.

1. Restate the following sets of rules by using parentheses, braces, or brackets. In each case a single rule will suffice.
    For example, the following rules

$$a \rightarrow x$$
$$a \rightarrow x + b$$
$$a \rightarrow c$$

may be restated as one:

$$a \rightarrow \begin{Bmatrix} x(b) \\ c \end{Bmatrix}$$

a) $Z \rightarrow A$
$\quad Z \rightarrow C + D + E$
$\quad Z \rightarrow C$
$\quad Z \rightarrow A + B$

b) $X \rightarrow a + b + c + d$
$\quad X \rightarrow a$
$\quad X \rightarrow a + b$
$\quad X \rightarrow a + b + d$

c) $X + A \rightarrow D + E$
$\quad Y + A \rightarrow C + G$
$\quad Y + A \rightarrow C + F$
$\quad X + A \rightarrow D + G$
$\quad Y + A \rightarrow C + E$
$\quad X + A \rightarrow D + F$

d) $Z \rightarrow A$
$\quad Z \rightarrow A + D + X$
$\quad Z \rightarrow A + D + Y$
$\quad Z \rightarrow A + Y$
$\quad Z \rightarrow A + R$
$\quad Z \rightarrow A + X$
$\quad Z \rightarrow A + R + S$

2. Which of the following forms is a terminal string for Language X according to Description 2 (Section 2.4): "i – b'a" or "i – p''a"? Which is predicted by Description 1? Write derivations for five possible forms of Language X in their terminal — i.e., phonetic — shapes from the rules given above.

3. Write derivations for five different terminal strings from the following grammar.

Initial string: Z

1. $Z \rightarrow A + B$

2. $B \rightarrow \left\{ \begin{array}{l} C + A \\ D \left\{ \begin{array}{l} R + A \\ S \end{array} \right\} \end{array} \right\}$

3. $A \rightarrow t + b$
4. $t \rightarrow a$, the
5. $b \rightarrow$ unicorn, house, flea
6. $R \rightarrow$ to, near, toward
7. $C \rightarrow$ bit, looked + at, fled
8. $D \rightarrow$ went, flew, trotted
9. $S \rightarrow$ home, away

4. Consider the following grammar:

Given: Z

1. $Z \rightarrow B(C)$

2. $B \rightarrow \left\{ \begin{array}{l} S(T)(U) \\ D(E) F \end{array} \right\}$

3. $S + T + C \rightarrow S + T + I$

4. $C \rightarrow (C) \left\{ \begin{array}{l} H \\ J(K) \end{array} \right\}$

Indicate which of the following strings are terminal strings derivable from the grammar, which are nonterminal strings of the grammar, and which are not derivable (ungrammatical). Concatenation signs are omitted.

a) *B*	g) *EK*	m) *SUJKJKJKI*
b) *STUI*	h) *BC*	n) *JKDEF*
c) *DE*	i) *SU*	o) *STHJHHJ*
d) *DF*	j) *STI*	p) *SHHJHHH*
e) *STJK*	k) *STJ*	q) *EFK*
f) *STUJK*	l) *ST*	r) *BCCJK*

5. Write a recursive grammar for the language mentioned above that consists of all and only the strings of the form *ab, abab, ababab,* and so on.

6. Write a grammar for the language with the terminal vocabulary *a, b, c* in which any string of any length of any combination of one or more of these elements is permitted.

7. Write grammars for the following languages (from Chomsky, 1957):

a) Every string is of the form *ab, aabb, aaabbb,* and so on, i.e., any number of *a*'s followed by the same number of *b*'s.

b) Every string is of the form *aa, bb, abba, baab,* and so on, i.e., any string of *a*'s and *b*'s followed by the mirror image of the same string.

8. Write a grammar for the language in which every string is of the form *abc, aabbcc, aaabbbccc,* i.e., *n a*'s plus *n b*'s plus *n c*'s. Hint: use a rule of the form $xy \rightarrow yx$.

9. Write a set of rules to produce the following (slightly simplified) Finnish noun paradigms:

	Singular	*Plural*	*Singular*	*Plural*
NOMINATIVE	talo *house*	talot	pöllö *owl*	pöllöt
GENITIVE	talon	talojen	pöllön	pöllöjen
PARTITIVE	taloa	taloja	pöllöä	pöllöjä
COMITATIVE	taloine	taloine	pöllöine	pöllöine
ESSIVE	talona	taloina	pöllönä	pöllöinä
TRANSLATIVE	taloksi	taloiksi	pöllöksi	pöllöiksi
ABESSIVE	talotta	taloitta	pöllöttä	pöllöittä
INESSIVE	talossa	taloissa	pöllössä	pöllöissä
ILLATIVE	taloon	taloihin	pöllöön	pöllöihin
ELATIVE	talosta	taloista	pöllöstä	pöllöistä
ADESSIVE	talolla	taloilla	pöllöllä	pöllöillä
ALLATIVE	talolle	taloille	pöllölle	pöllöille
ABLATIVE	talolta	taloilta	pöllöltä	pöllöiltä

Compare the nouns *tyyny*, partitive singular, *tyynyä*, illative singular, *tyynyyn; pannu*, partitive singular, *pannua*, illative singular, *pannuun*. Compare also as possibly related data the following participles for three different verbs: *antanut, pessut, tullut* with the stems *anta-, pes-,* and *tul-*.

CHAPTER THREE

PHRASE-STRUCTURE RULES

3.1 Immediate Constituents

Phrase-structure rules form a counterpart in the theory of generative grammars to two techniques of linguistic analysis, one old and one rather new. The old practice is the schoolroom drill of parsing, that is, of assigning grammatical labels to parts of a sentence. In a schoolroom drill the following analysis might occur:

The	*man*	*gave*	*me*	*a*	*book*
article	noun	verb	pronoun	article	noun

whole subject		indirect object	direct object

whole predicate

The other technique — in reality only a more sophisticated version of parsing — is so-called immediate constituent (IC) analysis. It attempts to break down constructions into subparts that are in some sense grammatically relevant. In analyzing the sentence above, we ask whether it is composed first of all of *the man* and *gave me a book*, or of *the man gave* and *me a book*, or perhaps of *the man* and *gave* and *me* and *a book*. Each of these analyses can be represented in several ways. We shall consider two of them. The last alternative might be represented thus:

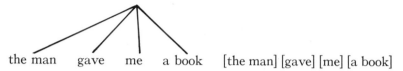

the man   gave   me   a book   [the man] [gave] [me] [a book]

We can combine labels such as those used in parsing with nodes in a "tree" or with the brackets for a representation of the "phrase structure" of the sentence. Thus, the first (most usual) analysis could be continued in more detail as follows:

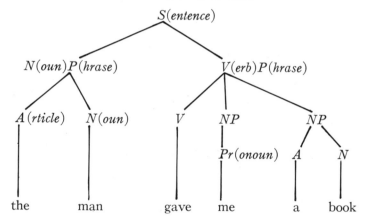

Or, equivalently:

```
[  [  [the]  [man]   ]
 S NP A   A  N    N NP

   [  [gave]  [  [me]  ]   [  [a]  [book]  ]   ]   ]
 VP V    V NP Pr  Pr NP NP A  A N    N NP VP S
```

A great deal of effort and discussion has gone into the question of how to choose among alternatives like the ones given above (see, for instance, Wells, 1947; Gleason, 1961; Longacre, 1960). For the present we shall not concern ourselves with this question but ask instead: What restrictions must be placed on grammatical rules so that they will yield the kind of information provided in the representations above? What are the consequences of the theory of grammatical structure inherent in such rules? How do such rules fit into a complete grammar for a language?

3.2 Restrictions on Phrase-Structure Rules

Phrase-structure (PS) rules* are again of the form $X \rightarrow Y$ and obey the following restrictions:

1. They are string-replacement rules (see Section 2.4) which replace the symbols to the left of the arrow if and only if the actual symbols occur in the final line of a developing derivation.

2. They are expansion rules, that is, rules which replace a single symbol by one or more symbols (one-many rules). In other words, the string to the left of the arrow may consist of either a single symbol or more than one. But if the rule has more than one symbol on the left, the symbol to be replaced must be flanked by concatenation signs and contain no instances of a concatenation sign. The replacing string may consist of one or more elements but must consist of at least one symbol (which is not null); that is, no deletions are permissible in PS rules. Similarly, the rewritten element may not be null.

3. No rules of the form $xy \rightarrow yx$, nor a series of rules having the effect of a rearrangement (permutation) of elements are permitted.

4. No rules of the form $A \rightarrow A + B$ (or $A \rightarrow B + A$) may be used.

In the formal theory of grammars a distinction is made between two types of PS grammars and rules, namely, context-free (CF)

---

* Several other designations are current, among them "constituent-structure rules," "IC rules," "immediate constituent structure expansion rules," "rules of formation." I prefer the original designation chiefly because it preserves the connection with the term "phrase marker" (P marker), to be discussed in Section 3.3, and because the abbreviation CS is used for context-sensitive grammars.

and context-sensitive (CS) grammars (see Section 7.4). As the names suggest, in the first type, the X of a rule $X \rightarrow Y$ must be a single symbol. In the second type, X may include the necessary context in which the change is to be brought about (the rule may, of course, be of the form $a \rightarrow b$ in env. $Z—W$). Since context-sensitive rules are practically indispensable for the description of natural languages in a simple way, we shall be concerned mainly with sets of rules having this possibility. (All of the examples and problems of Chapter 2 conform to the first restriction above. The reader should determine which of the examples also obey the other restrictions, that is, which of them are PS rules in the sense defined.)

3.3   Phrase Markers from Derivations

The effect of these restrictions is to provide sets of rules from which derivations can be written in which it is always possible to tell where elements "come from" by examining the successive lines. PS rules, then, will yield the kind of information provided by "trees of derivation" or labeled bracketings such as were given at the beginning of this chapter.

Let us consider a derivation from the set of rules given in Problem 3, Chapter 2:

1. Z
2. $A + B$
3. $A + D + R + A$
4. $t + b + D + R + A$
5. $t + b + D + R + t + b$
6. $a + b + D + R + t + b$
7. $a + b + D + R + the + b$
8. $a + unicorn + D + R + the + b$
9. $a + unicorn + D + R + the + flea$
10. $a + unicorn + D + toward + the + flea$
11. $a + unicorn + flew + toward + the + flea$

Evidently, our ability to reconstruct the "derivational history" of this terminal string depends on a process of matching succeeding lines in the derivation. Suppose we look at two successive lines in a derivation — that is, the ith line and the $(i + 1)$st line. We compare the left-most elements (delimited by +) in each line. If they are the same we proceed to the next element on the right in each string and compare. This process is continued until we reach the first pair which does not match. At this point we have reached the left-most part of the string replaced in the ith line and the left-most part of the string which has replaced it in the $(i + 1)$st line. The same process of matching is carried out from right to left until we reach the right-most elements of the replaced and the replacing strings. If the derivation is a proper phrase-structure derivation, the two elements reached in the first (ith) line will be identical. Every element from (and including) the left-most re-placing element to (and including) the right-most one is **derived from** the replaced element. This relation can be represented by writing the replacing string below the replaced element and drawing a line from each element in the replacing string to the replaced element (or, equivalently, by placing a pair of brackets around the replacing elements with the replaced element as its label). In the example given above, for instance, we can match the third and fourth lines and determine that the string $t + b$ is de-rived from A (i.e., "is an A" in this derivation from this grammar):

$$
\begin{array}{ccc}
A & & [\,t + b\,] \\
\diagup\diagdown & \text{or} & A \qquad A \\
t \quad\;\; b & &
\end{array}
$$

Now, suppose that in going from one line to the succeeding line, more than one element is replaced. If there were in the grammar, say, a rule

$C + A \rightarrow bit + the + unicorn$

then there would appear in a derivation succeeding lines containing the segments

$A + C + A$
$A + bit + the + unicorn$

If such were the case, then there would be two ways of relating the lines:

In such a derivation it is no longer possible to construct a unique derivational tree, that is, it is no longer possible to have the segments of our terminal strings "defined" as to their syntactic class for the purposes of our grammar. For this reason Restriction 2 is necessary in a PS grammar, which was after all designed precisely to provide the sort of structural analysis given by derivational trees. For this reason also, a derivation must proceed from line to line by the application of a single rule.

Now let us consider the third restriction, which excludes the permutation of elements in PS rules. Such permutations are theoretically possible in context-sensitive grammars (but not in context-free grammars) by a series of rules of the following sort. (See Chomsky, 1959a; for an attempt to formulate a restriction to meet this difficulty, see Chomsky, 1963; see also Section 7.4.) Suppose we wish to change a string $a + b$ into the string $b + a$. To do this directly in a single rule would clearly violate Restriction 2. But the following rules, which taken one by one do not transcend this limitation, will yield the same result:

$$a + b \rightarrow B + b$$
$$B + b \rightarrow B + a$$
$$B \rightarrow b$$

However, in the representation of the structure of the strings produced by such rules, b will be derived ultimately from a and a from b. Such a consequence is obviously unacceptable in a grammar for a real language. For instance, if we have PS rules which bring about a rearrangement of nouns and verbs, verbs will be analyzed as nouns and nouns as verbs whenever this switch is carried out in a derivation. We cannot avoid this difficulty merely by allowing no context-sensitive rules, except at the cost of considerably complicating our grammatical theories.

Restriction 4 states that there should be no rules which change an element into itself plus another element. Consider the steps in a derivation from a grammar with the rules $A \rightarrow A + B$, or $A \rightarrow (A)B$, and strings in which A occurs, say, to the left of an element C:

$$A + C$$
$$A + B + C$$

Again we do not know whether B is derived from A or from C. (That it is derived from one of them follows from the general restriction that no elements may be derived by a rule from the null element.) We can, however, bring about the same effect by a series of rules which will ensure that we can always construct a unique tree:

$$A \rightarrow (A')B$$
$$A' \rightarrow A$$

Rules of the form $A \rightarrow B + A + C$, on the other hand, are permissible. (Why?)

It will be recalled that such rules as the last few provide the necessary recursive property for a grammar. Because of the above difficulty (and other more serious ones), we shall see that the recursive property of a grammar is usually best built in not by PS rules, but by transformations.

A representation of immediate constituent structure for a string, such as is given by a labeled bracketing or labeled tree, is called a **phrase marker** (P marker). A P marker represents just that information from equivalent derivations (omitting irrelevant information such as the order of development for the various parts of the string) which enables us to tell where the parts of the string come from. Thus, to say that *the furious unicorn* is a noun phrase in the sentence *The furious unicorn laid its head in the virgin's lap* is to say that the phrase in question can be traced without remainder back to a node labeled "noun phrase" in the P marker constructible from the derivation of the sentence. The same string may be the result of several different derivations, even sometimes of derivations associated with different P markers. For instance, the German sentence *Das ist natürlich genug* may be an instance of two different structures:

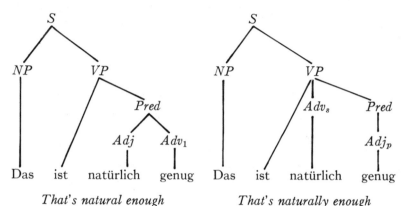

That's natural enough   That's naturally enough

(Adv_1 is a class of adverbs that modify adjectives; Adv_s is a class of sentence adverbs.) Or the English sentence *We saw the unicorn in the cornfield* may be represented in either of two ways depending on its derivation and its differing meanings more or less equivalent to 'In the cornfield we saw the unicorn' and 'We saw the unicorn that was in the cornfield.' Such instances of strings that may be represented by several P markers illustrate what is called **constructional homonymity.** * Where several different P markers may be associated with the same string, the string will be ambiguous (perhaps only in a very minor way, as in the sentence *I was writing the letter to my wife*). The fact of this ambiguity must be accounted for by the grammar.

To reiterate the important points, a P marker is always relative to a particular set of equivalent derivations from a particular grammar, and the structure of a terminal string cannot be repre-

---

* It is important to keep this notion distinct from the cases considered above in which it was impossible to determine a unique P marker from a single derivation.

sented by a one-dimensional segmentation alone (i.e., without some such device as labeled brackets).

3.4   Tagmemic Formulas and PS Rules

If we interpret tagmemic formulas as parts of generative grammars, that is, as sets of rules (and it is not at all clear that they should be so interpreted), they provide a notational variant to context-free PS grammars. The equality sign "$=$" is equivalent to the arrow. Symbols preceded by "$+$" (i.e.. obligatory units) are equivalent to any unparenthesized elements on the right of a rewriting rule. (The differing use of the plus sign in the two systems must be sharply emphasized. In tagmemic notations it is a prefixed operator signaling the obligatory status of an item in a construction. There is no overt concatenation sign.) Symbols preceded by "$\pm$" (optional elements) are equivalent to parenthesized elements in a PS rule, and symbols separated by "$/$" are equivalent to elements within braces. The colon between the so-called "slot name" and "slot-filler name" is again equivalent to an arrow. (A few other symbols used occasionally will be ignored here.) Thus, the tagmemic formula

$$X = + A:a + B:b \pm C:c/d/e$$

expresses exactly the same relations as the rules

$$X \to A + B(C)$$
$$A \to a$$
$$B \to b$$
$$C \to \begin{Bmatrix} c \\ d \\ e \end{Bmatrix}$$

The lists of members of the slot-filler classes would then be equivalent to rules of the form

$$c \to \begin{Bmatrix} c' \\ c'' \\ c''' \end{Bmatrix}$$

There is one minor advantage to the rewriting rules in the fact that the parentheses, braces, and so on, are pairs of enclosing symbols which make it possible to build more depth into a single rule. For instance, compare the two following statements:

$$A \rightarrow B\left(C\left(\begin{Bmatrix} e \\ f \end{Bmatrix}\right)\right) \qquad \begin{aligned} A &= + B \pm X \\ X &= + C \pm e/f \end{aligned}$$

Here the more "linear" tagmemic representation makes it necessary to set up an intermediate symbol X to take care of the parenthesized parentheses of the rewrite rule. On the other hand, the use of the colon makes possible the collapsing of several rules into a single line, a notation that is not possible in PS rules.

A more serious objection to the tagmemic notation has to do with what is presumably the central notion of tagmemic theory, namely, the necessary distinction between a "slot" and a "filler" by means of the colon (:). In the reformulation in rewrite rules this connection will always be represented by a simple rule changing one nonterminal symbol into another. The P markers for strings produced from such rules will always have branches of the form (for a formula $X = + A:a$):

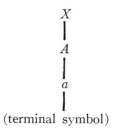

(terminal symbol)

Although, as we shall see, it is sometimes advantageous to build in an intermediate node (for purposes of transformational manipulations), it is by no means desirable to have to do this for every nonterminal symbol, as is required by the tagmemic notation.

The lack of context-sensitive rules leads to serious complications, as can be seen from the following example. Suppose we have a construction (X) consisting of two parts (A) and (B). Some members of A can occur with all members of B, while some members of A can occur only with certain members of B. Examples from natural languages come readily to mind. Restrictions of this sort are easily handled by context-sensitive rules:

1. $X \rightarrow A + B$
2. $A \rightarrow \begin{Bmatrix} A_1 \\ A_2 \end{Bmatrix}$
3. $A_2 + B \rightarrow A_2 + B_2$
4. $B \rightarrow \begin{Bmatrix} B_1 \\ B_2 \end{Bmatrix}$

A grammar with no context-sensitive rules can produce the same strings:

$$X \rightarrow \begin{Bmatrix} A_1 \begin{Bmatrix} B_1 \\ B_2 \end{Bmatrix} \\ A_2 + B_2 \end{Bmatrix}$$

However, we have lost the information that A_1 and A_2 are included in the same class A and that B_1 and B_2 are included in B, information that may be of crucial importance for the rest of the grammar. To preserve this analysis we must postulate two types of X's:

1. $X \rightarrow \begin{Bmatrix} X_1 \\ X_2 \end{Bmatrix}$
2. $X_1 \rightarrow A + B$
3. $A \rightarrow A_2$
4. $B \rightarrow B_2$
5. $X_2 \rightarrow A + B$
6. $A \rightarrow A_1$
7. $B \rightarrow \begin{Bmatrix} B_1 \\ B_2 \end{Bmatrix}$

Here, not only do we have to carry out the same replacement several times and postulate (an otherwise irrelevant) distinction between X_1 and X_2, but we must make sure that the A's and B's resulting from X_1 do not pass through the later rules. (Some of the objections raised above have been obviated by the most recent presentation of tagmemic theory in Elson and Pickett, 1962. But the basic points of the slot-symbol and class-symbol description and the lack of context-sensitive rules remain untouched. For a detailed comparison of various recent descriptive frameworks, including tagmemics, see Postal, forthcoming.)

3.5   Phrase Structure for Language X

Most of the considerations which bear on the possible ways of setting up PS rules for a language have to do with subsequent parts of the grammar, mainly with transformational rules. We shall present a fuller discussion of such "analytical" questions in Chapter 5. By way of illustration, however, let us describe a further part of Language X and then put down a set of PS rules for this hypothetical language.

Language X has two types of inflected words, nouns and verbs. Nouns are inflected for two numbers, singular and plural, and two (or three) cases, that is, there are two overt case markers, nouns functioning as subject being unmarked. Verbs are divided into three syntactic classes: those which take no objects (intransitives) and those (transitives) which govern each of the two cases (call them case x and case y). All verbs exhibit number concord with the subject, while transitive verbs also show number concord with the object. Inflection is by suffixation with the exception of the object number marker on the verb which is prefixed to monosyllabic verb stems, otherwise infixed after the first syllable of the verb stem. There are two morphological classes of nouns, determined by the fact that the number suffixes show different forms for these two classes (nonautomatic). (Before going on, the reader may wish to organize this information into a set of PS rules.)

Initial string: $\# S \#$

1. $S \rightarrow Nom + VP + SM$

2. $VP \rightarrow \begin{Bmatrix} Verb_i \\ NP + Verb_t \end{Bmatrix}$

3. $Verb_t \rightarrow (IS)OM + Verb_{tr}$

SM: *subject marker*
i: *intransitive*
t: *transitive*
IS: *initial syllable*
OM: *object marker*

4. $Verb_{tr} \rightarrow \begin{Bmatrix} Verb_x \\ Verb_y \end{Bmatrix}$

5. $NP(IS)OM \begin{bmatrix} Verb_x \\ Verb_y \end{bmatrix} \rightarrow Nom \begin{bmatrix} x(IS)OM + Verb_x \\ y(IS)OM + Verb_y \end{bmatrix}$

6. $Nom \rightarrow Noun \begin{Bmatrix} Sg \\ Pl \end{Bmatrix}$

7. $SM \rightarrow SMSG$ in env.

$$\# Noun + Sg \begin{Bmatrix} Verb_i \\ Noun \begin{Bmatrix} Sg \\ Pl \end{Bmatrix} \begin{Bmatrix} x \\ y \end{Bmatrix} (IS)OM \begin{Bmatrix} Verb_x \\ Verb_y \end{Bmatrix} \end{Bmatrix} - \#$$

8. $SM \rightarrow SMPL$

9. $OM \rightarrow OMSG$ in env. $Sg \begin{Bmatrix} x \\ y \end{Bmatrix} (IS)-$

10. $OM \rightarrow OMPL$

11. $Noun \rightarrow \begin{Bmatrix} Noun_1 \\ Noun_2 \end{Bmatrix}$

12. $Noun_1 \begin{bmatrix} Sg \\ Pl \end{bmatrix} \rightarrow Noun_1 \begin{bmatrix} Sg_1 \\ Pl_1 \end{bmatrix}$

13. $Sg \rightarrow Sg_2$

14. $Pl \rightarrow Pl_2$

At this point, additional rules would provide the actual forms involved for the various inflections and bases.

The initial string for this grammar is given in the form $\# S \#$. All sentences produced by the rules will be marked at either end by a boundary marker, $\#$. Such a technique is useful for identifying elements occurring in various positions in the string (e.g., an initial X can be identified as $\# X$). The double-cross is a terminal symbol and it has a special property: it is not derived from any element. Occasionally, the initial string of a grammar is given in the form $\# S \# S \# S \# \cdots$ or $\# S \#\# S \#\# S \# \cdots$ to indicate that an indefinite number of initial S's is available, each bounded by a sentence boundary marker. (In terms of our "derivation machine" of Section 2.5, the machine is now able to tell when it has reached the end of the string being scanned.)

The rules are arranged in such a way that they may be applied one after the other whenever applicable without the necessity of returning to an earlier rule, although a single rule may be applied several times when necessary (but compare Section 3.8). For example, the verb phrase (VP), which may contain further instances of the noun, is developed before the latter is expanded. In general, rules that apply to a class of items should be placed before the rules that split the class into smaller subclasses, since if the other order is followed the general rule can be applied only by naming each of the subclasses involved. For instance, Rule 3, which expands transitive verbs into an optional initial syllable, an obligatory object marker and a verb stem (or remainder of a stem for polysyllabic verbs — see Section 3.6 for a discussion of this unsatisfactory handling of a discontinuity), must be placed before Rule 4, or else both types of transitives must be named. Similarly, the distinction between the two morphological subclasses of nouns is delayed to the end to simplify the rules.

Care must be taken to ensure that unwanted recursion (looping) does not occur. Thus, if Rule 3 were formulated

$$Verb_t \rightarrow (IS)OM + Verb_t$$

all derivations would be caught up at this point into a never-ending expansion

$$Verb_t$$
$$OM + Verb_t$$
$$OM + OM + Verb_t$$
$$OM + OM + OM + Verb_t \cdots$$

(This formulation, of course, would also violate Restriction 4.) It is this necessity to change symbols which causes the proliferation of special symbols in a generative grammar. Much can be done in the way of making a set of rules easier to follow. We shall consider some of these (nonsystematic) devices in Section 3.7.

Such problems result from the decision to make a theory as precise and explicit as possible. Indeed, one value of an explicit theory is that inconsistencies and wrong formulations are shown up in sharpened detail. For instance, the statement that any adjective in English can be compared by adding *-er* and *-est* and that the resultant forms are also adjectives is tantamount to a recursive series of rules that would generate such forms as "sloweresterer":

$$Adj \rightarrow Adj \begin{Bmatrix} er \\ est \end{Bmatrix}$$

$Adj \rightarrow slow, pretty, big$, etc.

In other words, the compared forms of adjectives in English are not "adjectives" but "compared adjectives" or the like.

Rules 7 through 10 and 12 through 14 illustrate again the ordering of "special" and "elsewhere" statements (here, the choice is purely arbitrary). The rules could be simplified by taking one of the "allo-forms" from the beginning (perhaps in its final morphophonemic shape, if there is no danger of confusing it with homonymous forms). The advantage of following the procedure used here is that in transformational rules it will be possible to refer to the whole class, say *OM*, since the rules define *OMSG* and *OMPL* as coming from this source. Conversely, Rule 6 as stated makes it necessary to refer to both *Sg* and *Pl* when making statements about the number of nouns. An intermediate step

$$Nom \rightarrow Noun + Num$$

$$Num \rightarrow \begin{Bmatrix} Sg \\ Pl \end{Bmatrix}$$

would build this general term into the phrase structure (and P markers).

The use of abbreviated symbols is, of course, not a logically necessary part of the theory. We might instead use such symbols as *Sentence, Nominal, Verb phrase, Subject marker*. It is easy to see, however, that this would greatly increase the length of the rules, and, especially in the case of complex transformational rules, make the statements hard to follow. If, in addition, we use such verbal formulations as "is composed of" (for →), "either ··· or else" (for braces), and so on, many of the statements would be extremely complicated. (As an example, the reader may wish to translate Rule 7 in all its detail into ordinary English.)

3.6 Some Inadequacies in PS Rules

The rules for the phrase structure of Language X point up several difficulties in a grammar conforming to the adopted restrictions. One such difficulty appears in the handling of the object marker affix in polysyllabic verbs. Because of the restrictions on PS rules, it is necessary to take care of this alternation of position in a highly artificial way. The position of the object marker depends only on the more-or-less haphazard shape of the transitive verb stem. However, to take care of this alternation it is necessary to set up an optional element which does not stand for any syntactically relevant unit (as do most of the other elements). The optional element (IS) simply stands for the accidental list of "initial syllables" in polysyllabic transitive verb stems. The remaining part of these stems must then be put in (replacing $Verb_x$ and $Verb_y$) by means of clumsy and inefficient context-restricted lexical rules. For instance, for a stem *kli-pi* of type $Verb_x$ there would have to be rules like these:

$$IS \rightarrow kli\text{-}, \cdots \text{ in env. } - \begin{Bmatrix} OMSG \\ OMPL \end{Bmatrix} Verb_x$$

$$kli\text{-} \begin{bmatrix} OMSG \\ OMPL \end{bmatrix} Verb_x \rightarrow kli\text{-} \begin{bmatrix} OMSG \\ OMPL \end{bmatrix} pi$$

Such a treatment — which would be something like introducing the English noun stem /mæn/ in two stages as /mæ–/ and /–n/ — is clearly wrong. The transitive verb stems should be introduced as units in the lexical rules. The object marker should be introduced as a prefix, allowing the independent selection of monosyllabic and polysyllabic stems. And the infixation of the object marker after the first syllable of a polysyllabic verb stem should be brought about by a low-level rule in the grammar. But such a rule, which would rearrange items in the string, is beyond the scope of PS rules. Clearly, something besides PS rules must be included in an efficient grammatical theory.

    For the same reasons we are prevented from producing the proper selections for the subject marker in a simple way. It is easy to see that a rule like 7 would be greatly complicated in a more realistic grammar, for the environment specified in Rule 7 includes all the sequences that have been derived from *VP* at that point in the rules. If Rule 1 were stated as follows:

$$S \rightarrow Nom + SM + VP$$

then we could produce the proper form by a rule with only the relevant environment specified:

$$Sg + SM \rightarrow Sg + SMSG$$

Once again, a low-level rule might place the subject marker at the end of the sentence.

In order to state such a rule, however, we would have to go beyond the limits of PS rules in several ways besides the violation of Restriction 3 (which excludes permutations). First of all, since PS rules must always specify in detail the elements in the strings to which they apply, we would again be forced to specify all the possible strings occurring between the subject marker and the end of the sentence (as in Rule 7). Second, since we have changed *SM* into two different shapes to agree with the subject noun, we must mention both of these forms. That is, even with rules that do not conform to Restriction 3, we would have to spell out in detail something like the following rule (assuming no more complexities in the verb phrase than we have given):

$$
\begin{bmatrix} SMSG \\ SMPL \end{bmatrix}_1 \quad \begin{bmatrix} Verb_i \\ Noun \begin{bmatrix} Sg \\ Pl \end{bmatrix} \begin{bmatrix} x \\ y \end{bmatrix} (IS)OM \begin{bmatrix} Verb_x \\ Verb_y \end{bmatrix} \end{bmatrix}_2
$$

$$
\rightarrow \begin{bmatrix} Verb_i \\ Noun \begin{bmatrix} Sg \\ Pl \end{bmatrix} \begin{bmatrix} x \\ y \end{bmatrix} (IS)OM \begin{bmatrix} Verb_x \\ Verb_y \end{bmatrix} \end{bmatrix}_2 \begin{bmatrix} SMSG \\ SMPL \end{bmatrix}_1
$$

Such a rule would be greatly complicated in a grammar for a language in which the subject marker might take on many more forms (such as a Bantu language). What we want is some kind of formalism which will enable us to make a simple rule corresponding to this: place the subject marker (whatever its final shape may be) at the end of the verb phrase (no matter what particular form it may have). That is, a rule such as

$$SM + VP \rightarrow VP + SM$$

in which the symbols *SM* and *VP* are no longer understood to mean the actual symbols in this shape, but rather whatever is a subject marker and whatever is a verb phrase in the grammar. Such rules, which are called transformations, will be studied in the next chapter.

3.7   On Writing Readable Rules

One of the fundamental aims of transformational theory has been to construct a general theory that will make it possible to choose between two alternative grammars for a language on some formal basis. One of the features posited for such an evaluation has been simplicity, identified with the total number of symbols used in the grammatical rules of a theory. (We have tacitly assumed this criterion above, for instance, in choosing between two different arrangements for a set of rules.)

There is another kind of simplicity, however, which is nonsystematic and has to do rather with the practical problem of stating a theory in such a way that it is easy to follow. The following suggestions are offered in the hope that they will lead to more readable presentations of grammatical theories.

A name is only a name, and the labels and symbols for a set of rules may be arbitrarily chosen (as long as different symbols are used for different points in the structure of rules).* From a theo-

---

*   I am ignoring here the important question of the possibility that at least some of the designations for syntactic classes will be supplied by general linguistic theory, i.e., by a set of universal categories like "noun," "verb,"

retical point of view even digits might be used, and for a machine they would be quite as satisfactory as anything else. For the human reader, on the other hand, alphabetic designations are preferable. They should be chosen with a view to their mnemonic value, and the source of this value should always be given where it is not obvious. It is much easier to remember what *SM* means and how it functions if we are told that it stands for "subject marker."

Since the elements of a set of rules are defined by their further development in the rules, it is helpful to follow some rational scheme for changing the symbols as the elements pass through successive replacements. For instance, it is a common practice to use lower-case letters for (PS) terminal representations, capitals for nonterminal. One scheme might be to start off with all capitals and then symbolize the approach to terminal items by using more and more lower-case letters. *VB, VRB, Vb, Vrb, Verb* illustrates a series in which successive developments are signaled not only in this way but also by using less and less abbreviated designations. In particular, it would be extremely useful to use a special way of marking — say, by underlining — those items which undergo no further developments before the lexical replacements. It is annoying to have to skim through a long lexical list which turns out not to have the symbol you are looking for, and then to be forced to look through numerous rules to see what happens to the item (sometimes hidden in a complex set of contexts). Needless to say, any such scheme should be stated for the reader and not left to his talent for a "discovery procedure."

The emphasis on concise formulation, which has resulted from transformational theory, should be applied to the rules themselves and not to a presentation of them for the reader. Here, any kind

---

and so forth. The differences between languages have been stressed so much in recent years that we tend to overlook the very real similarities. It is quite true that "verb" does not mean the same thing (in terms of categories of inflection, and so on) in discussing, say, Japanese grammar and English grammar. On the other hand, it is just as true that Japanese verbs parallel English verbs in many ways, and there is no need to apologize for calling both classes by the same name.

of explanatory additions that help the reader to follow the rules and to understand the reasons for their particular form should be included, either by way of marginal definitions (e.g., for special symbols), comments interpolated between the rules, or in the form of a summarizing paraphrase of the rules. Above all, examples should be given. Nothing is easier than to fall into the error that the reader will be as familiar with your special notations as you are. Nothing is more formidable than a page bristling with rules and unfamiliar symbols. (For an example of a step-by-step presentation of a set of rules with interpolated comments, see Lees, 1960.)

One of the chief reasons for analyzing in one way rather than another in the PS rules is the usefulness of the nonterminal symbols for stating transformational relations between various sets of sentences. Therefore, it would be a worthwhile practice to list the transformations in which a general symbol is mentioned at the first introduction of the item. This practice would at the same time provide for the reader (and the writer!) a quick check on the merits of his analysis.

3.8   Ordering of PS Rules

I have assumed that the PS rules are strictly ordered in such a fashion that a terminated derivation can be produced by moving through the rules only once. Other assumptions are possible.

We might assume that the PS rules are **cyclically ordered,** that is, a derivation is produced by going through the rules from first to last. Then, if any nonterminal symbols remain in the string, we again go through the whole series of rules. This process is continued until all the symbols in the string are terminal. Such an arrangement is necessary if certain kinds of recursion are brought about by PS rules: if, for instance, the initial symbol (S) can occur again within a string on the right-hand side of some rule. This view brings with it certain consequences. We must extend our notion of a grammar to include a method for examining a string and comparing each symbol to a list of nonterminal (or terminal) symbols in order to see whether the string must be sent back through the rules. Alternatively, we must assume that the grammar can carry along the information as to whether the string has undergone a change in a complete run-through of the rules. Only when such a complete run-through (with no change) has taken place will the derivation terminate. Decisions about the role of the transformational rules will have an obvious bearing on whether or not we adopt such a cyclical ordering (e.g., do we attribute *all* recursive processes to the transformational rules?). Such an ordering is assumed in Chomsky, 1956.

On the other hand, it might be assumed that the PS rules are completely unordered (as in various adaptations of PS grammars for machine translation). If the rules are not ordered, then it is impossible to have rules corresponding to statements like this: "Such and such an item appears in the form x in this environment, in the form y everywhere else." We would then have to specify in detail all the environments included in "everywhere else." (The reader may wish to restate some of the ordered sets of rules given above and in the preceding chapter in this way.) The effect of such an assumption is to force all kinds of low-level (e.g., morphological) detail high into the rules, or to make it necessary to list not only the irregular formations but also all the regular ones (e.g., in the rules for noun inflection in Section 2.4). The assumption of an ordering of some kind is, in fact, quite in keeping with most grammatical descriptions both traditional and modern.

Problems for Chapter 3

At this point the reader may wish to work through some published examples of PS rules (e.g., Lees, 1960; Chomsky, 1962a; Harms, 1962).

1. Construct P markers (both in the form of trees and in the form of labeled bracketings) for three terminal strings from the grammar of Problem 3, Chapter 2.

2. How could the rules for Language X (Section 3.5) be restated so as to allow the choice of *SMSG* or *SMPL* before *VP* is developed?

3. Rewrite the PS rules for Language X to take care of the following additional details:

a) There are some nouns which cannot appear in the plural.
b) There are some nouns which cannot appear in the singular.
c) Among the verbs governing case x there are some which require number concord between the object noun and the subject noun.
d) In all three groups of verbs there are some which can appear only with a subject belonging to one subclass of those nouns which can have both a singular and a plural.
e) There is a negative particle which appears optionally after the verb. When this particle is present *all* transitive verbs require case y on their objects, and intransitive verbs require case y on the subject.

4. Write PS rules for the following sets of strings:

a) E B
E D B R
E D B
E B R
E D B S
E B S

b) kore wa hon desu
kono hon wa akai
kore wa akai hon desu
kono hon wa akai desu
kore wa akai
kore wa akai desu
akai desu
hon desu
kore wa hon ja nai
kono hon wa akaku nai
kore wa akai hon ja nai
kore wa akaku nai
akaku nai
hon ja nai

c) a a d
a c f
b a g
b c h
c a i
b b d
a b e
c b j
c c d

d) filius puellam amat
filii puellam amant
filium puella amat
filium puellae amant
filios puellae amant
filios puella amat
filius puellas amat
filii puellas amant

e) a b c b
a d c d
a f c f
a b a d c d c b
a d a f c f c d
a b a f c f c b
a d a b c b c d
a f a d c d c f
a f a b c b c f
a b a b c b c b
a f a f c f c f
a d a d c d c d

f) en mann   *a man*
mannen   *the man*
menn   *men*
mennene   *the men*
en kone   *a woman*
konen   *the woman*
koner   *women*

huset   *the house*
hus   *houses*
husene   *the houses*
en stor mann   *a big man*
den store mannen   *the big man*
store menn   *big men*
de store mennene   *the big men*

konene	*the women*	en stor kone (etc. like *mann*)
et tre	*a tree*	et stort tre *a big tree*
treet	*the tree*	det store treet
trær	*trees*	store trær
trærne	*the trees*	de store trærne
et hus	*a house*	et stort hus (etc. like *tre*)

5. Write a PS grammar (omitting Restriction 3) for the language (from Chomsky, 1957) *aa, bb, abab, baba, aabaab,* and so on, i.e., an arbitrary string of *a*'s and *b*'s followed by a repetition of the same string. Hint: use a boundary element and context-sensitive rules.

6. Outline a set of rules for a language in which every sentence consists of a noun followed by a verb followed in turn (for some verbs) by another noun. Nouns are divided into the following classes: abstract and concrete. Concrete nouns are divided into animal, vegetable, and mineral nouns; animal nouns are divided into human and nonhuman. For each major type of verb (i.e., those which do and those which do not take a second noun as object) there are some verbs which are unrestricted as to the co-occurring nouns, some which are restricted as to the class of the co-occurring nouns, with all possibilities represented (e.g., verbs with abstract subject and human object, verbs with concrete subject and human object, verbs with mineral subject and animal object, and so forth).

CHAPTER FOUR

GRAMMATICAL TRANSFORMATIONS

4.1 Linguistic Levels

So far we have not considered the central and distinctive notion
of the grammatical transformation, a concept which has given
transformational theory its name. A grammar which conforms to
the general description of a linguistic theory as given so far is simply
a generative grammar (within the limitations of Section 3.2, a PS
grammar). Only those theories which contain a level of rules of the
type to be discussed in this chapter are transformational grammars.
Before proceeding to this discussion, let us consider briefly the
general idea of a linguistic level.

In somewhat vague terms, a level may be considered as a system
of symbols, rules, and so on, to be used for representing utterances.
To represent utterances on the phonetic level we make use of a set
of symbols strung together according to certain conventions:
some symbols occur in linear order, other symbols may be placed
above or below certain of the linear symbols. Or in a phonetic
theory making use of distinctive features, an utterance may be
represented by a matrix of pluses and minuses, each column
standing for a linear segment of the utterance, each row indicating

a particular distinctive feature, its presence in the particular segment being symbolized by a + in that column.

New levels are introduced into a grammatical theory in order to simplify the statement of grammatical restrictions. For example, it would be extremely cumbersome on the level of phonemic representations to account for the fact that the starred item does not occur in English:

/low/   /lówliy/   /lówliynis/
/slow/   /slówliy/   */slówliynis/

Whereas with morphemic representations (or some such "higher" level, perhaps PS rules) such restrictions can be easily handled.

Each **level** of a linguistic theory comprises the following parts: a set of **primes** (i.e., atoms or indivisible elements), a set of **relations** (including =) some of which with the primes make up an underlying combinatorial system or "algebra" for the level, a set of **markers** to be associated with or to represent utterances on the given level, and finally, in a multileveled theory such as is necessary for describing a natural language, a set of relations between the representations on that level and the representations on other levels of the theory. (For a more precise and detailed account, see Chomsky, 1955b, Chapters 2 and 5.)

In the preceding chapter we were concerned with setting up such a level of representation (in an informal way). There the primes were the single elements or symbols (delimited by +) occurring in the rules and derivations. Among the relations of the PS level were such relations as the one symbolized by the arrow, "follows from," "is a," and so on. The markers were the P markers, and the whole apparatus of rules and conventions governing their use, methods of deriving markers, and so on, was constructed to allow the representation of utterances on the level of phrase structure.

In our conception of general linguistic theory, a level in a linguistic description is characterized by the types of rules permitted, that is, by certain of the relations that form part of the definition of the level. This usage should be carefully distinguished from that of other linguistic theories, otherwise much confusion will result. A comparison with the system described in Chapter 3, for instance, will show that there is no fixed set of "levels" such as word level, clause level, phrase level, sentence level in the systems of PS rules and P markers. Similarly, the levels of phrase structure, transformations, and phonology are not based primarily on a difference in the nature of the linguistic aspects or substance to which they refer as are, for instance, the divisions in some discussions (such as H. L. Smith, Jr., 1962) into levels of phonology, morphology (i.e., "grammar" in the older narrower sense), and semology. In our usage, "level" refers primarily to the structure of grammatical theories (and implicitly to the structure of language).

(The word "level" is also used occasionally in another sense to refer to the ordering of rules within a single level and also to the ordering of the PS, transformational, and phonological rules with respect to each other. Thus a "high-level" rule is a rule that is placed earlier in an ordered list than a "low-level" rule, and a PS rule is a rule of a "higher level" than a phonological rule.)

At several points in the preceding chapter it was seen that PS rules were clumsy or inadequate. The next step is to inquire whether further levels of representation might not be necessary or desirable in a linguistic theory. Let us first sketch the characteristics of one such level and the type of rule embodied in it, and then consider some of the further reasons for setting up a transformational level.

4.2 Transformations

A **transformational rule** (T rule) may again be considered a rule of the form

$$X \rightarrow Y$$

although, as we shall see, it is usually not put in quite this format. This time, however, X and Y do not stand for simple strings. Instead, they stand for classes of P markers, i.e., terminal strings from the PS component of a grammar, together with their structural description by labeled trees or bracketings (or, as we shall see, strings of terminal elements with new "derived" P markers). Transformational rules may delete parts of a P marker, rearrange them into a new order, add new items, and make several such changes at once.

In other words, a transformation is a rule which requires us or allows us to perform certain changes in the terminal strings of the PS grammar if, and only if, the string has a certain structure. This structure must be precisely what is represented in the P marker of this string as derived in a certain way from a particular set of rules.

The difference between PS rules and T rules can be made clearer, perhaps, by the following remarks. The difference between a word and what is denoted by a word is ordinarily very clear. When we are talking about words, however, many confusions can result if the distinction is not kept clear, and various devices are used to indicate that we are talking about a symbol rather than what it symbolizes: the word John, "John," *John.* " 'John' is a four-letter word" and "John is my friend" are perfectly legitimate sentences. What would result from transposing the single quotes to the word *John* in "John is my friend" would be either false or nonsense. Now, strictly speaking, PS rules should all be stated in the following way

$$\text{``}S\text{''} \rightarrow \text{``}NP\text{''} + \text{``}VP\text{''}$$

That is, this rule is not an instruction to replace a sentence by a noun phrase plus a verb phrase (whatever that would mean), rather it says "Replace the symbol S in the next line of the derivation by the symbol NP concatenated with the symbol VP." On the other hand, a T rule which includes the symbol NP (say) is not referring to the actual symbol NP but rather to whatever is an *NP* (in the sense defined in Chapter 3). Consider a copy editor who is told to go through a manuscript and replace all French words with English words. If he interprets this instruction as a PS rule he will go through the manuscript and replace the phrase "all French words" by the phrase "English words." If he interprets it in a way analogous (but not precisely equivalent) to the instruction of a transformation, he will reach for his French-English dictionary.

As we shall see, the relationship between T rules and PS rules not only gives us solid reasons for setting up a PS component at all, but also provides a powerful tool for deciding how to set up the PS rules (i.e., how to analyze sentences) for a particular language.

Transformational rules are stated in the following way. Each rule must be marked as either optional or obligatory. The first part of the rule is a **structural description** (SD, also called **structural analysis** or **structure index**) specifying the class of strings (in terms of their analysis by P markers) to which the rule applies. Thus a T rule for Language X as described in Section 3.5 might apply to all sentences with transitive verb phrases:

$$SD: Nom - NP - Verb_t - SM$$

The rule would then apply to an indefinite number of terminal strings which could be subdivided into four parts traceable one after another to the nodes of the P markers specified above. Often the structural description contains variable symbols such as X or Y, standing for any strings (usually including null as a possible value). For instance, if only the two items NP and $Verb_t$ were of interest in the T rule and we wished to allow for various other possibilities in the rest of the string, we might give the structural description as follows:

$$X - NP - Verb_t - Y$$

The second part of the rule specifies the **structural change** (SC) by means of variable signs (such as X) with subscript numbers or simply numbers referring to the segments specified by the structural description. In this example, X_3 (or 3) would refer to whatever is a $Verb_t$ in the string.

Finally, it is occasionally necessary to state various conditions that must be met in addition to those specified in the structural description. For instance, suppose in a transformation applying to transitive sentences in Language X it were necessary to restrict the transformation to those strings in which the subject and object nouns were not identical. We might then add a condition:

$$\text{where } X_2 \neq X_1 \begin{Bmatrix} x \\ y \end{Bmatrix}$$

(i.e., where the second segment is not a repetition of the first segment plus a case symbol).

As an example we may take the rule that is cited most often as a prototype of a transformational relation, namely, the passive transformation. It is given (in Chomsky, 1957, p. 112) as follows:

> *Passive* optional
> Structural analysis: $NP - Aux - V - NP$
> Structural change: $X_1 - X_2 - X_3 - X_4$
> $$\rightarrow X_4 - X_2 + be + en - X_3 - by + X_1$$

The rule may be paraphrased thus: A passive may be formed from any string that may be analyzed without remainder into four parts: (1) a noun phrase followed by (2) the auxiliary (i.e., the complex of elements leading to past tense, person marker, modals, and so on) followed by (3) a verb (actually a verb of a certain class must be specified) followed by (4) a second noun phrase. The passive counterpart to each such sentence is formed by switching noun phrases (X_1 — the first segment of the analyzed string — and X_4), by attaching $be + en$ (the past participle formant) to the auxiliary, and by placing *by* before the last noun phrase. For instance, the string with the following P marker fits the structural description:

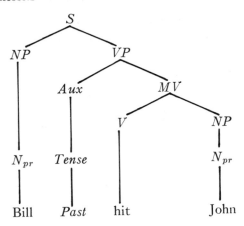

It may be transformed into the passive string:

$John + Past + be + en + hit + by + Bill$

i.e., *John was hit by Bill.* On the other hand, the PS rules must be set up in such a way that the string *Bill + Past + go + home* will not undergo the passive transformation (i.e., so that *home* in this string is not an *NP*). The product of a transformation is referred to as a **transform.**

Sometimes T rules are given in an abbreviated form simply by placing the changed items of the structural description to the right of an arrow:

$$NP - Aux - V - NP' \rightarrow NP' - Aux + be + en - V - by + NP$$

Here, it is necessary to distinguish between different instances of the same type of item by numbers or other marks as above (*NP* as against *NP'*). Occasionally a double arrow $\Rightarrow$ is used to underline the difference between T rules and the simple rewrite rules of the PS component.

As these examples show, T rules do not apply to sentences in their terminal form but rather to the underlying abstract strings produced at a certain point in a grammar. For instance, in the analysis of English from which the example is taken, it is most

convenient to set up the items in the complex of verbal parts —
modals, suffixes, tense auxiliaries — in such a way that the suffixes
occur immediately before the bases to which they will eventually
be attached. Most transformations apply to strings in that order.
At a low level of the grammar the affixes are placed in the proper
position following their bases.

Transformations are often erroneously conceived to be direct
descriptions of processes that a speaker follows in constructing
sentences (the same statement holds for generative theories as a
whole). The investigation of how speakers actually construct or
understand sentences is properly the concern of psychology or
psycholinguistics. Although it is probable that a refined theory
of linguistic structure will be relevant to such a study, a grammar
does not provide a direct model for the speaker (or the hearer).
A transformation is basically a statement of certain relations
holding between structures in a grammar. It is introduced because
such a rule can do things which simpler rules cannot do (or can
do only in a clumsy manner). In the case of an optional transformation, it is a statement that if strings of such and such a form
are representations of grammatical sentences in a language, then
strings of such and such another derived form are also grammatical.
For example, the passive transformation states that if *Bill hit John*
is a sentence so also is *John was hit by Bill*, and if *The smokestack
was eating fried pies* is a sentence (of a given degree of grammaticality) so also is *Fried pies were being eaten by the smokestack*.
Further, this rule states that our second passive example is the
passive transform of the second active sentence and not of *Bill hit
John*. Without such a rule there would be no way to express this
special relationship.

Other transformations might express similar connections between
Bill hit John and any of the following sentences:

Who hit John?
Who(m) did Bill hit?
Did Bill hit John?

It was John that Bill hit.
For Bill to hit John (was inexcusable).
(Bill went off in a huff) to hit John.
Bill's hitting John (was a shock).
(I saw) Bill hit John.

Further, by way of the passive T rule we reach sentences like these:

Who was hit by Bill?
That John was hit by Bill (was a surprise).

It takes very little reflection to see that a PS grammar specifying each of these types independently would be enormously complicated.

As the last examples (and many others) show, T rules must operate in such a way that they can apply to already transformed structures. Thus the P markers to which they apply will come only partly from the PS rules directly. The product of a transformation will be a new derived P marker, capable of undergoing further changes (see Section 4.4).

4.3   Typical Uses for T Rules

The reasons for adding a set of transformations to a generative grammar have been sufficiently argued elsewhere (in Chomsky, 1957, and many other places). I shall confine myself here to outlining some of the typical situations calling for the use of T rules.

Whenever several sets of constructions occur in a language in each of which the same grammatical relations obtain (co-occurrence restrictions, government, concord, and so on) but where some difference (say, in order) makes it impossible to derive them at once from PS rules, the constructions should probably be related transformationally. That is, one set (the most convenient) should be taken as basic and the others derived by T rules. For instance, in German there are three basic patterns with respect to the position of the finite verb (each being used in various different sentence types). In each pattern the whole network of dependencies of case government, co-occurrences of nouns with adjectives and verbs, and so on, is exactly the same. It would be extremely uneconomical to derive the patterns separately. Instead, two of the arrangements are produced by various transformations (see Bach, 1962a). The passive in English and some other languages offers a similar example as do the various constructions involving nouns and adjectives (in the following examples and throughout this book, starred examples are strings presumed to be ungrammatical):

This house is new.	The new house · · ·
The man is young.	The young man · · ·
*The house is young.	*The young house · · ·

Such examples (involving co-occurrences of major base types) may strike the reader as being beyond the bounds of purely grammatical description. But on the one hand it is easy to find examples that are well within the bounds of traditional linguistic description in the narrowest sense:

He is my friend.	I consider him my friend.
They are my friends.	I consider them my friends.
*He is my friends.	*I consider him my friends.

And on the other hand it seems to be impossible to delimit in any satisfactory and general way (i.e., to cover not only English but also, say, Chinese and Eskimo) what is properly a "structural" or grammatical restriction and what is some other type ("semantic" or "semological"). In any case, the categories and restrictions of a transformational grammar can be made as crude (or as subtle) as those of any other grammatical description.

Whatever can be done only in a very clumsy or artificial way by means of PS rules (for instance, the discontinuities in Language X as treated in the last chapter) is best left to a transformational rule (or possibly morphophonemic rules). Thus, in Estonian the case government of verbs could be handled by long and complex context-restricted rules in the PS component (there are fourteen cases in Estonian). However, the same result can be accomplished by two extremely simple obligatory transformations (see Harms, 1962).

Among the optional transformations there are some which operate on two strings at once, conjoining them, embedding one into another, forming conjunctions, and so on. Such rules are called **generalized** (or two-string) **transformations**. These are of particular importance, since they provide the recursive characteristic which we have seen to be necessary in a grammar. It is true that recursion can be provided in PS rules. In many situations, however, the use of recursive PS rules leads to unsatisfactory results. Let us consider two such situations.

In English there is no upper limit to the number of adjectives that can be strung together before a noun. Suppose we account for this fact by a series of steps in our PS rules of the following sort:

1. $NP \rightarrow T(A)\ Noun$ *T: article*
2. $A \rightarrow Adj\ (Adjt)$
3. $Adjt \rightarrow A$
4. $Adj \rightarrow$ *long, black,* etc.

Because of Restriction 4 (Section 3.2) we cannot write Rule 2 as $A \rightarrow Adj\ (A)$. This would lead to derivations from which unique P markers would not be constructible. Hence it will be necessary to allow backtracking to a previous rule if we are to allow for an indefinitely long series of adjectives before the noun. But it is neater not to have to provide for exceptions to the general instruction that rules are to be applied strictly in their listed order (with a possibility of repeating one rule several times when applicable). Suppose that the above rules were nevertheless incorporated in a grammar (i.e., that we assume a cyclical ordering). Then a phrase

like *the long black formidable submarine* would be assigned the
following P marker:

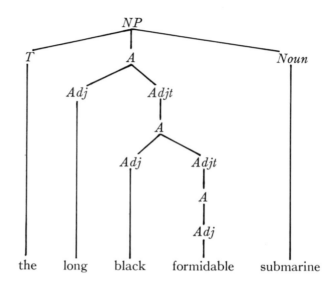

But both our intuition about English structure and the demands of
simplicity tell us that this is far too much "structure" for a simple
coordination of attributive adjectives. Instead, the proper analysis
should show something like this:

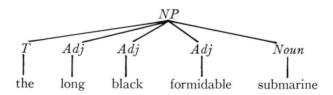

This last structure, however, can be provided by PS rules only if
some upper bound is given to the series of adjectives (i.e., by a
nonrecursive rule). However, the desired analysis can be easily
given by means of T rules (this example based on Lees, 1961a; for
English adjective rules see Carlota S. Smith, 1961).

Consider next the case of sentences such as this: *He went down-*

town (in order) to buy a trunk. A PS rule for such a sentence might take this form (much oversimplified):

$$S \rightarrow NP + VP \ ((in\ order)\ to\ VP)$$

But here again there is no upper bound to the length of the construction: *He went downtown in order to buy a trunk in order to pack his things in order to take them to Taiwan* · · · . And the statement of the co-occurrence restrictions between the *NP*'s and *VP*'s must be carried out infinitely many times to prevent such sequences as **He went downtown in order to entail great difficulties in order to be abundant in order to be my friends* · · · . These facts of co-occurrence can be neatly provided for by a transformation of the following general form:

$$\left. \begin{array}{l} NP + VP \\ NP' + VP' + X \end{array} \right\} \rightarrow NP + VP + in + order + to + VP' + X$$
where $NP = NP'$

The example is again much oversimplified. Here the identity of the two *NP*'s ensures that the proper restrictions are carried over from the underlying simple strings.

Sentences which are derived from PS terminal strings by the application of obligatory transformations only and phonological rules are called **kernel sentences**. The usefulness (and supposed basic nature) of the distinction between kernel sentences and derived sentences has been called into question (by Schachter, 1962b). Whether or not it is basic and just how to make the decision as to what belongs in the set of kernel sentences hinges on another question, namely, the problem of weighting various parts of the grammar in arriving at a measure of simplicity. The general answer is clear: we choose those strings as belonging to the kernel which lead to the simplest over-all grammar. The problem is quite parallel to the problem of choosing basic morphemic alternants (as discussed, for instance, by Bloomfield, 1933, pp. 217–219).

★4.4   Derived P Markers*

A rule of grammar may perform any of the following operations:

deletion: $a + b \rightarrow b$ (or $a \rightarrow null$)
replacement: $a \rightarrow b$
expansion: $a \rightarrow b + c$
reduction: * $a + b \rightarrow c$
addition: $a \rightarrow a + b$
permutation: $a + b \rightarrow b + a$

Since PS rules can carry out only a part of these operations, and
T rules may perform any of them in any combination, it would
seem that T rules are inherently more powerful than PS rules;
that is, T rules can do anything which PS rules can do, but not
vice versa. The reader may test the first part of this statement
by rephrasing a set of PS rules as T rules:

$SD: \# - S - \#$
$SC: X_1 - X_2 - X_3 \rightarrow X_1 - NP + VP - X_3$

Whether this statement is true not only in terms of the permitted
operations but also for the classes of languages that can be generated by the two types of grammars is a theoretical question
that has not been solved. However, since T rules apply to P
markers rather than to simple strings, the effect of a replacement
made by a PS rule differs from the effect of what is nominally the
same operation carried out by a T rule. That is, a PS rule $a \rightarrow b$
will extend a branch terminating in b to the node labeled a,
whereas a transformational replacement will replace the node a
(together with whatever is derived from it) by the node b (with
whatever is derived from it), as in the following representations
for a string with the initial shape $a + c$:

---

* Sections preceded by a star may be glossed over on a first reading and
returned to later for more careful study.

effect of a PS replacement   effect of a T replacement

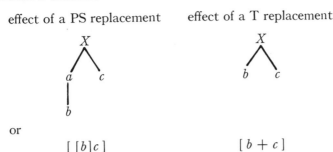

or

$$[\,[b]c\,]$$
$$Xa\ a\ X$$

$$[\,b+c\,]$$
$$X \qquad X$$

This difference must be borne in mind when considering whether to produce a certain item by a T rule or a PS rule.

With this last bit of discussion we come to an important general question. T rules have been characterized as rules in which P markers are changed into new P markers. What we want to state are a few general principles telling us just how these new P markers are formed, given a P marker and a certain type of transformation. (To supplement the following informal discussion of what are still not completely solved problems, see Chomsky, 1955a; 1955b, Chapter 8; and 1961a.)

First, let us make some general remarks about P markers. A proper P marker (when represented in tree form) is a topological structure of lines and nodes conforming to the general requirement that a unique path be traceable from the termination of every branch to the point of origin of the whole tree (or for that matter from any node to any other node). Further, the relation symbolized in the tree diagram by the spatial arrangement from left to right of the branches emanating from a node must be preserved in the arrangement from left to right in the strings represented by the tree (though not necessarily in the sentences ultimately derived from the string). That is to say, there are no lines which cross each other

nor substructures of the form

Nor are there any branches of the form

Or, rather, this last diagram is equivalent to

(Analogous remarks may be made about labeled bracketings.)

Let us now informally define two relations holding between parts of P markers. As a preliminary step let us define the **derivational path** of a symbol X in a P marker as the sequence of symbols occurring on the unique path leading from the origin or root of the tree to (and including) X. Now we may say that a symbol X is **part of** a symbol Y if Y occurs in the derivational path of X. Thus every symbol is part of itself. We may extend the notion to cover a sequence of several symbols and say that several symbols are **jointly part of** another symbol if each one is part of the symbol and none are parts of each other. Finally, we say that a symbol A **dominates** one or several symbols X, Y, and so on, when X, Y, and so on, are (jointly) part of A and the only other symbols that are part of A are related to one or another of X, Y, and so on, by the relation *part of*. These notions are exemplified in the following tree:

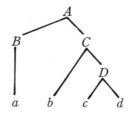

Here the derivational path of a is (A, B, a); the derivational path of A is (A); of D is (A, C, D). Further, a is part of (and dominated by) B; a is part of (but not dominated by) A; a together with b, or a together with D, are jointly part of A; A dominates $A, B + C$, $a + b + c + d$; C dominates $b + c + d$; a dominates a, and so on. It is clear that if X dominates Y, Y is part of X but not necessarily vice versa. "Dominates" is thus the converse of the relation "is a" (in the sense of syntactic class membership) discussed in the previous chapter. "Part of" is an extension from the concept "derived from" also discussed in the preceding chapter. (More careful definitions of these terms would be given in terms of the underlying derivations; see Chomsky, 1959a, 1961a.)

Now let us consider each of the types of changes that may be effected by a T rule.

DELETION. This is the simplest type of change to describe. In a deletion the item is simply removed from the P marker together with any nodes that it dominates and any nodes dominating it. (Lines not terminating in a label are automatically removed.) For example,

$SD: X - Y - Z$
$SC: X_1 - X_2 - X_3 \rightarrow X_1 - X_3$

This rule would make the following kind of change in the P markers to which it applied:

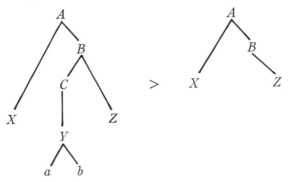

(Here > symbolizes "becomes by a structural change.")

Examples of T rules of this sort are the rules that carry the strings underlying such sentences as *John was eating a ham sandwich* into *John was eating; He can derive the sentence* into *He can;* or *He's cooking supper in the kitchen* into *He's cooking in the kitchen*.

Each of the next three types of transformations (simple replacement, expansion, and reduction) may be considered as being of one basic type, which replaces part of a P marker with a new P marker. In each type the P marker of the replacing item is inserted at the place of the replaced P marker in such a way that the new element is part of every node of which the old element was a part (except for the old node itself).

SIMPLE REPLACEMENT.

$$SD: X - Y - Z$$
$$SC: X_1 - X_2 - X_3 \rightarrow X_1 - W - X_3$$

If Y and W are terminal elements the change will be simply as follows:

If Y and W are nonterminal, i.e., more complicated structures of branches and nodes, the whole structure dominated by W is put in place of the whole structure of Y.

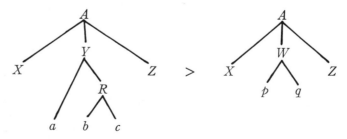

The extension to the case where one or the other (but not both) are terminal elements should be obvious.

EXPANSION.

SD: $X - Y - Z$
SC: $X_1 - X_2 - X_3 \rightarrow X_1 - R + S - X_3$

For example:

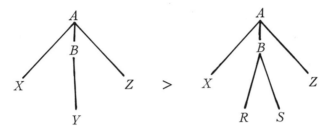

If there were no intermediate node (B) R and S would, of course, be connected to A.

REDUCTION. This relation is simply the converse of the foregoing. In the derived P marker one item takes the place of several in the original P marker:

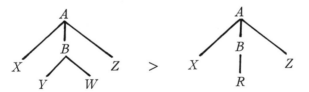

Typical examples of the foregoing types are the many transformations in which a sentence (or a transformed version of a sentence) is put into some part of another sentence. In such rules the "embedding" sentence is called the **matrix** sentence, the embedded one the **constituent** sentence (or string). One such rule forms the

sentence *I know that my Redeemer liveth* from the strings underlying,
say, *I know the fact* and *My Redeemer liveth*:

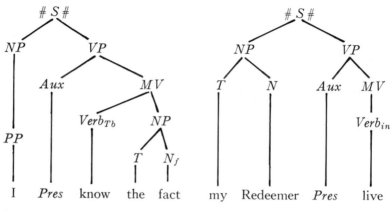

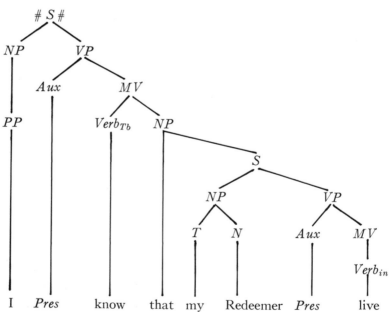

ADDITION. In all of the preceding types something in the first
P marker is replaced by another P marker (or null); hence the

point of attachment is clearly defined. The cases to be considered now are less neat. The difficulty may be seen in the following instance. Suppose we have a transformation of the following form:

SD: $X - Y - Z$
SC: $X_1 - X_2 - X_3 \rightarrow X_1 - X_2 - R - X_3$

And suppose further that this rule applies to P markers of the following shape (among others):

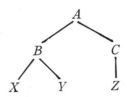

The point of insertion in the terminal string is clear enough. But to which node should R be attached in the derived P marker? That is, which of the following forms should the P marker take?

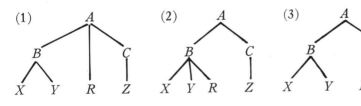

As a case in point, consider the two transformations that have been suggested for English to form sentences like *Can he come?* and *He can't come* from the string underlying *He can come*, i.e., $NP - C + M - X$ (where C is the verbal suffix, M stands for modals like *can, will, must,* and so on). The structural description for both rules is the same, the change for the first being $X_1 - X_2 - X_3 \rightarrow X_2 - X_1 - X_3$, for the second $X_1 - X_2 - X_3 \rightarrow X_1 - X_2 + n't - X_3$ (see Chomsky, 1962a, p. 141). Now on the one hand it would be desirable to assume that *n't* is attached to the modal (i.e., is connected to the node M) so that the question transformation will cover this case also to yield *Can't he come?* and the like. But if the derived P marker shows that *can* + *n't* is an *M*, then the rule can be reapplied to yield the ungrammatical sequences *He* + *can* + *n't* + *n't* + *come*, *He* + *can* + *n't* + *n't* + *n't* + *come*, and so forth. The solution here seems to be a reformulation in such a way that *not* occurs in the PS rules, and the reduced form *n't* is produced from *not* (see Lees, 1960). There does not seem to be any *generally* satisfactory solution to such problems as yet, although suggestions for various special cases have been made.

Two points applying to both addition and replacement transformations must be borne in mind. First, the items which are added or substituted must either be constants (i.e., terminal items) or else fully formed P markers from some source. That is, we want our rules to be set up in such a way that we do not have to go back through the PS rules to derive new items for the transforms. Second, the possibility that transformations may reapply to the transform must be kept in mind. In some cases the rules must be stated in such a way as to allow recursion, in other cases not (as in the example of the last paragraph). The possibilities of recursion are especially great when general variable symbols are used. For instance, suppose we want to allow for the addition of some type of modifier, say, *S* before a certain construction, *R*. If we write a rule such as the following

$$X + R + Y \to X + S + R + Y$$

where *X* is a variable, then the outputs of the rule can be reanalyzed (with *S* now included in *X*) as *X* + *R* + *Y*, and the string can go through the rule again. The difficulty of such cases often makes it preferable to put such an item into the PS rules.

PERMUTATIONS. In a transformation producing a rearrangement of various parts of the P marker, the principle followed in arriving at the new P marker is to carry out the change in the original P marker in such a way that the rearranged items remain *part of* the lowest nodes possible, consistent with the restrictions on proper P markers as sketched above. For example:

SD: $X - Y - Z$
SC: $X_1 - X_2 - X_3 \rightarrow X_2 - X_1 - X_3$

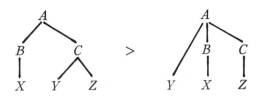

The foregoing remarks must be taken as suggestions for the sort of general principles that must be worked out for the derivation of new P markers by transformations, rather than as definite solutions. The statement of general rules of this type demands a good deal more formal apparatus than we are using in this exposition. (About the only extended discussion of these problems is to be found in the as-yet-unpublished work of Chomsky, 1955b and 1955a.) At the moment it is often necessary to make *ad hoc* additions and definitions in a set of T rules. Definite solutions will only be forthcoming after the consequences of various suggestions have been tried out in detailed descriptions.

As an example of the kind of problem posed, consider the rule which carries a sentence like *Henry went away* into *Away went Henry;* i.e., the P marker (simplified)

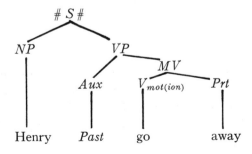

into some other P marker by a rule of roughly the form

SD: $NP - Aux - V_{mot} - Prt$
SC: $X_1 - X_2 - X_3 - X_4 \rightarrow X_4 - X_2 - X_3 - X_1$

Now, depending on whether we consider the switch of subject to end position (1) or the switch of the particle to front position (2) as occurring first (by the general rule for permutations given above) two different derived P markers are possible:

(1)   (2)

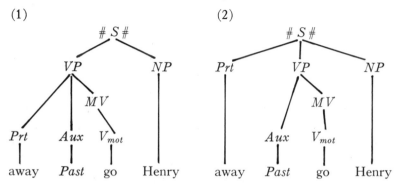

Here, it would appear that the second alternative works out better, since the *VP* of the first alternative does not have the range of possibilities of most *VP*'s, e.g., we cannot attach *to* or *ing* for a nominalization (**to away go*) as we can with most verb phrases. And in fact, when transformations are defined carefully (in terms of underlying elementary transformations which map each term of the analyzed string into some term of the resultant string from left to right), the second alternative is automatically given.

The two fairly clear cases are those in which a deletion is performed and those in which an element (or several elements) is substituted for something already in the P marker. It is partly for this reason that very often "dummy" elements are set up in the PS rules to provide a point of attachment for the inserted elements. One way out of some of the difficulties we have been considering would be to use fuller P markers to describe the changes brought about by a T rule. If, for instance, we want to specify that the agent phrase produced in the passive transformation is part of the verb phrase, is itself a prepositional phrase, and that *be + en* is part of the auxiliary, we might state the rule in some such form as this:

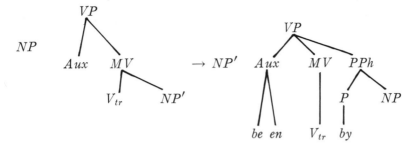

Something like this is, in fact, implied in statements such as "this element [*be* + *en*] is considered as part of Aux$_2$" (Lees, 1960, p. 34).

As we have seen, the PS rules provide the definitions for the parts of the strings that may undergo various changes in T rules. However, most published versions of transformational grammars have also had to define certain symbols in the course of the transformational developments. These special definitions must be kept in mind when evaluating an analysis. When a set of T rules has recourse too often to the device "Let $X = \{a, b + c, y(z)\}$" or the like, this usually indicates that the job of revising the PS component in the light of the T rules (and vice versa) has not been carried out sufficiently. Perhaps the general rule for evaluating such analyses should be to restate them in such a way that every such definition is built into the PS component. For instance, an analysis which has the definition

Let $Af = Z_1, Z_2, Z_3, \emptyset, Past, en$

should be considered equivalent to (and evaluated as) one in which the node Af is built in at each such point. Or such a use of special definitions should, perhaps, be considered as a method for abbreviating a number of special transformations (as a convenience to the reader) and the evaluation should be made in terms of the individual rules so abbreviated. If some such stipulations are not made in evaluations, it will always be possible to simplify a set of rules trivially by defining some special symbol to stand for a complex set of alternative structures.

T rules cannot be considered to be ordered in the same sense as PS rules. Consider the sentences:

Being hit on the head is unpleasant.

Hitting people on the head is considered bad taste.

Both sentences have in their transformational history (part of their "T markers") the application of the passive transformation and a nominalizing transformation (which attaches *ing* to a sentence), but in a different order. In the first sentence the passive has been applied first to one of the underlying strings, which has then been nominalized. In the second sentence the nominalization has provided the object for a string (*People – consider – bad taste – hitting people on the head*) which has then undergone the passive transformation.

Yet it seems unlikely that T rules are completely unordered. For instance, in German there are a number of permutational transformations which rearrange items that have been set up in a rigid order in the PS rules. The subject is identified by its initial position in the string for purposes of verbal suffix government. Case government of verbs similarly requires a rigid ordering (to prevent, for example, **Ich habe das Mädchen dem Bild gezeigt*, 'I showed the girl to the picture'). For this reason, we assume that the rules for government, and so on, take place before the shift rules. This is again a general problem of transformational theory that needs further investigation. Perhaps T rules can be set up in "fields" in such a way that any order of application within each field is permissible. Reentry into a field, however, would be impossible once a string had been put through a rule in some later field.

4.5   Some T Rules for Language X

After this rather abstract discussion of some of the problems connected with the transformational component, let us return to a more concrete exemplification of the apparatus of T rules by describing a few hypothetical rules for Language X. In thinking through T rules, it is useful to begin by stating in the clearest language possible the relation between various candidates for underlying and derived strings. Many parts of transformational descriptions turn out to be formalized analogues to statements long made in traditional presentations of grammar in language classes, pedagogical texts and so on. Examples are the passive that is presented as an operation on an underlying active sentence and the preposing of long attributive constructions in German from an underlying relative clause.

First let us revise the PS rules for Language X (Section 3.5) by omitting some of the details that can be handled more easily outside such rules. Thus, we may circumvent the division of poly-syllabic transitives into an initial syllable and a remainder by striking the symbol *IS* wherever it appears. We must now add a low-level obligatory transformation that will transpose the object marker and the first syllable for verbs of more than one syllable. From Chapter 2 (Section 2.4) it will be recalled that we have in-cluded in the roster of phonemes for Language X a special syllable boundary marker $/-/$, which can be used to good advantage here.

T obligatory, placement of Object Marker

$$X + NP + OM + Y - Z + SM + W$$
$$\rightarrow X + NP + Y - OM - Z + SM + W$$

Condition: $Y, Z \neq$ null, Y does not contain $-$

(It should be noted that "$-$" is being used here as a symbol of the strings undergoing the rule, not as a means of marking off segments of the structural description, as in previous examples.) If the selection of proper subject markers is carried out as suggested in Section 3.6, then the rule just given must follow the rule (also transformational) which places the subject marker at the end of the verb phrase.

Rules 11 to 14 are similarly concerned with a low-level alter-nation that is not syntactically relevant. The reader will have discovered that the additional detail of Problem 3, Chapter 3, necessitated a rather complicated elaboration of this morphological detail. Let us therefore also remove these rules from the PS rules, this time not to be taken care of by a T rule but rather by a morphophonemic rule (see Chapter 6).

We shall now consider the formation of sentences of Language X corresponding to the types *John and Bill went downtown, I see John and Bill,* and so on. There is no upper limit to the number of nouns that may be conjoined in this way. The conjoining particle is *ku*. It stands between the nouns conjoined and replaces any case marker that may be present in the noun preceding it — in other words, the last noun in the series is the only one which shows the case of the whole series. When a series of conjoined nouns take the subject position, the subject marker on the verb must take the plural form. A similar statement holds for the object marker, except when the negative particle is present, in which instance the object marker remains singular unless one of the object nouns is plural. What we want is some kind of conjunction transformation of roughly this form:

$$\left. \begin{array}{l} \dot{X} + \dot{Noun} + Y \\ X + Noun' + Y \end{array} \right\} \rightarrow X + Noun + ku + Noun' + Y$$

But various details must be accounted for. The case marker must be deleted on the first noun. Possible changes in the subject and object markers must be provided for. Since the agreement between subject and subject marker and between object and object marker has to be taken care of in such a rule (or subsequently), we are led to consider the possibility of accounting for these agreements by some other means than the PS rules as given in the previous chapter. (Additional transformations like the English passive in which some change is made in the subject and object would also speak for this revision.) We might then tentatively eliminate those rules from the phrase structure. Similar considerations might also lead us to eliminate case government rules from the PS component. In fact, the case morphemes might be set up as separate constituents coming from the verb. They could then be shifted by a low-level permutational rule to the proper position after the nouns (or last noun in a series). It would then also be possible to simplify the noun conjunction rule, since it would not be necessary to specify the deletion of the case markers in the first of a pair of conjoined nouns. Assuming that these changes are made and that the details of agreement and government are dealt with by further obligatory rules, the noun conjunction rule could be stated in substantially the form above. A little reflection will show that the rule does include the possibility of recursion so that an indefinite number of nouns may be conjoined.

Like many languages, Language X provides the possibility of embedding sentences as modifiers of nouns in larger structures. This is done in the following way. When two sentences contain instances of the same noun, one of the sentences may be put into the other as a direct modifier of the noun. This is done by deleting the noun, changing the object marker or subject marker (according to the function of the noun in the constituent sentence) in the embedded sentence to another form (called the "relative" subject or object marker) and placing the transformed constituent sentence directly before the modified noun in the matrix sentence. The whole construction functions then very much like a relative clause in English.

Considerations such as the above illustrate the way in which different parts of a grammatical theory must be built up by a process of tentative statement, addition of details, and modification of earlier decisions in the light of later ones. In the next chapter we shall consider in a little more detail the process of forming and testing hypotheses about grammatical structure.

Problems for Chapter 4

At this point the reader may wish to work through some published sets of T rules. Many additional limited problems for analysis may be found in such works as Nida, 1949; Gleason, 1955; Merrifield *et al.*, 1962.

1. Indicate which of the strings below are terminal strings of the grammar given, which are kernel sentences, and which, if any, should be "ambiguous."

Given: Z

1. $Z \rightarrow (Z') A + B$
2. $Z' \rightarrow Z$
3. $A \rightarrow \{L, M, N\}$
4. $\begin{bmatrix} L \\ M \end{bmatrix} B \rightarrow \begin{bmatrix} L + m \\ M + n \end{bmatrix}$
5. $B \rightarrow \{l, m, n\}$

a) $L + M + n + m$
b) $M + n + N + m$
c) $M + n + M + n$
d) $M + L + N + n + m + n$
e) $N + M + n + n$
f) $M + M + M + n + n + n$
g) $L + m + n + N$

T 1 (optional)
$$X + B + A + Y \rightarrow X + A + B + Y$$
T 2 (obligatory)
$$X + n + M + Y \rightarrow X + M + n + Y$$

2. Revise the PS rules for Language X (including the restrictions of Chapter 3, Problem 3) as suggested in Section 4.5. Then formulate explicitly the T rules necessitated by these revisions as well as the two optional rules suggested (noun conjunction and relative clause).

3. Restate the rules for English noun inflection given in Chapter 2 (Section 2.4) in such a way that the node *Af* is built in above each suffix.

4. Simplify your description of the Japanese sentences of Problem 4b, Chapter 3, by restating the PS rules and adding a few T rules.

5. Restate the rules for the Norwegian noun phrase (Problem 4f, Chapter 3) in the same way.

6. In the same way simplify the description of the Latin sentences (Problem 4d, Chapter 3) and at the same time account for the fact that the three-word sentences can occur in any order: e.g., *filius amat puellam, amat puellam filius,* and so on.

7. Write rules for the following Japanese verb forms.* Assume that only forms 1–4 are produced in the PS rules, 5–11 by T rules (here, merely indicate the partial replacements that occur). Thus, your solution should consist of three parts: PS rules, abbreviated T rules, morphophonemic rules (i.e., unrestricted rewriting rules like the rules of Section 2.4). Representations are morphophonemic (tu = [tsu], ti = [či], si = [ši]).

	eat	*see*	*wait*	*ride*	*meet*
1. NONPAST	taberu	miru	matu	noru	au
2. PAST	tabeta	mita	matta	notta	atta
3. TENTATIVE	tabeyoo	miyoo	matoo	noroo	aoo
4. PAST TENTATIVE	tabetaroo	mitaroo	mattaroo	nottaroo	attaroo
5. INFINITIVE	tabe	mi	mati	nori	ai
6. IMPERATIVE	tabe	mi	mate	nore	ae

---

* Based on Samuel E. Martin, *Essential Japanese*, rev. ed. (Rutland, Vt., Charles E. Tuttle Co., Inc., 1956).

	eat	see	wait	ride	meet
7. GERUND	tabete	mite	matte	notte	atte
8. CONDITIONAL	tabetara	mitara	mattara	nottara	attara
9. ALTERNATIVE	tabetari	mitari	mattari	nottari	attari
10. PROVISIONAL	tabereba	mireba	mateba	noreba	aeba
11. NEGATIVE	tabenai	minai	matanai	noranai	awanai

	talk	smell	write	call	read	die
1.	hanasu	kagu	kaku	yobu	yomu	sinu
2.	hanasita	kaida	kaita	yoɴda	yoɴda	siɴda
3.	hanasoo	kagoo	kakoo	yoboo	yomoo	sinoo
4.	hanasitaroo	kaidaroo	kaitaroo	yoɴdaroo	yoɴdaroo	siɴdaroo
5.	hanasi	kagi	kaki	yobi	yomi	sini
6.	hanase	kage	kake	yobe	yome	sine
7.	hanasite	kaide	kaite	yoɴde	yoɴde	siɴde
8.	hanasitara	kaidara	kaitara	yoɴdara	yoɴdara	siɴdara
9.	hanasitari	kaidari	kaitari	yoɴdari	yoɴdari	siɴdari
10.	hanaseba	kageba	kakeba	yobeba	yomeba	sineba
11.	hanasanai	kaganai	kakanai	yobanai	yomanai	sinanai

8. Write a grammar that will generate all natural numbers (0, 1, 2 · · ·) in the form # 0 #, # 1 #, and so on. Note that # 0 # is the only sequence that can begin with 0. Set your rules up in such a way that you can include an obligatory transformation supplying a comma between all triples (counting from the right) to yield, e.g., # 1, 000, 267, 394 #.

CHAPTER FIVE

PROBLEMS

OF SYNTACTIC ANALYSIS

5.1 Analytical Operations

Up to this point we have been concerned primarily with describing part of the apparatus of rules and distinctions necessary in a grammatical theory. The present chapter will be oriented more toward the data confronting the linguist. We shall consider various ways in which typical problems of linguistic analysis can be handled with the machinery so far developed. Like any other linguistic theory, transformational theory must be tested on a wide variety of languages. Actually, far more work has been done than is apparent from the bibliographies of published work, although much of it is difficult to obtain. Some languages that have been worked on from this point of view (partly in Master's theses and extensive term projects in courses) are English, German, Russian, Spanish, Hindi, Thai, Mandarin, Cantonese, Finnish, Estonian, Turkish, Japanese, Pangasinan, Tagalog, Arabic, Hidatsa, Mohawk, Luganda, Laz. A start has been made toward utilizing the framework of transformational theory for historical problems.

Let us begin by considering the following set of Japanese sentences (based on Lesson IV, Part II of the first book in the series *Hyōjun Nihongo Tokuhon* by N. Naganuma). The transcription is morphophonemic (see Problem 7, Chapter 4). Phonemic pitch accent, intonations, and juncture are omitted; conventional spacing is used.

1. doozo tatte kudasai
2. watakusi wa tatte imasu
3. doozo aruite kudasai
4. watakusi wa aruite imasu
5. doozo to o akete kudasai
6. watakusi wa to o akete imasu
7. doozo to o simete kudasai
8. watakusi wa to o simete imasu
9. doozo kosikakete kudasai
10. watakusi wa kosikakete imasu
11. doozo enpitu o totte kudasai
12. watakusi wa enpitu o totte imasu
13. doozo hon o mite kudasai
14. watakusi wa hon o mite imasu

In considering these utterances, we must first of all assume that they are grammatical sentences of the language. This assumption will not always be tenable. That is to say, in assembling data for an analysis a great deal of editing is usually done (see Hockett, 1958, pp. 142 f.). Real discourse — especially when spoken in a natural context — is always full of fits and starts and incongruities ("This form is found in Homer, don't we?"). In other words, we cannot identify the set of grammatical sentences with the set of actually occurring sentences. This statement, which seems obvious to the author, has given rise to a great deal of resistance. Probably this resistance is based on the linguistic habits of our culture. Linguists have had to fight long and hard to free the study of language from normative conceptions of grammar. But the decision to edit and possibly reject part of the given utterances has nothing in common with the prescriptivist's zeal. The difficulty stems, then, from the loaded meaning of a word like "grammatical" and the clearly laudable desire to keep linguistics on an objective, empirical basis. The situation is complicated by the cultural setting, but I do not think the difficulty can be circumvented simply by accepting the equation of "occurring" and "grammatical." What we describe with our grammar is a partially idealized system. To show how this system is used in actual discourse is a further problem. But we must be doubly on guard that our intuitions and theories are not biased because of our cultural training and the dimly remembered voices of the classroom (on these problems see Putnam, 1961).

Assuming, then, that we have a set of bona fide, well-formed sentences, we proceed to construct a set of rules to account for them. The set of sentences implies a grammar with as many minimal rules as sentences, each with the same left term:

Given: S
G_1: 1. $S \rightarrow$ *doozo tatte kudasai*
    2. $S \rightarrow$ *watakusi wa tatte imasu*

and so on. Our problem is to reduce this grammar to a simpler form.

We notice immediately that various pairs of sentences are partly identical. Stated abstractly, given two rules

$$X \rightarrow T_1 + T_2 + T_3 + \cdots + T_n$$
$$X \rightarrow T_1 + T'_2 + T_3 + \cdots + T_n$$

we can posit a rule

$$X \rightarrow T_1 \begin{Bmatrix} T_2 \\ T'_2 \end{Bmatrix} T_3 + \cdots + T_n$$

or if T'_2 is null

$$X \rightarrow T_1(T_2)T_3 + \cdots + T_n$$

The incorporation of such a rule, which will generate exactly the same set as the original pair, will simplify the description and amount, in effect, to a generalization about certain positional classes of the language. Generally speaking, except with carefully "precooked" data, there will be many conflicting ways of drawing rules together. For instance, with the three English sentences

John purchased a house
John lives in a house
John lives here

there will be two ways of analyzing the phrase *in a house*. With repeated trials and errors and the free use of any presystematic knowledge of the language, we choose the analyses which maximize the independence of the classes set up and which minimize the number of times various items need to be mentioned.

In the data before us, we can gather together all the odd sentences and all the even sentences, which match at each end, and account for the data by two rules:

$$G_2: 1. \quad S \to doozo \left\{ \begin{array}{l} tat \\ arui \\ kosikake \\ to + o \left\{ \begin{array}{l} ake \\ sime \end{array} \right\} \\ e\text{N}pitu + o + tot \\ ho\text{N} + o + mi \end{array} \right\} te + kudasai$$

$$2. \quad S \to watakusi + wa \left\{ \begin{array}{l} tat \\ arui \\ kosikake \\ to + o \left\{ \begin{array}{l} ake \\ sime \end{array} \right\} \\ e\text{N}pitu + o + tot \\ ho\text{N} + o + mi \end{array} \right\} te + imasu$$

Next, we observe that exactly the same list of items appears within the braces in the two rules. We incorporate this fact into our grammar by positing a class (or construction) X occurring at this point in our two types of sentences and describing its internal make-up only once:

$G_3: 1. \quad S \to doozo + X + te + kudasai$
$\quad\quad 2. \quad S \to watakusi + wa + X + te + imasu$

$$3. \quad X \rightarrow \left\{ \begin{array}{l} tat \\ arui \\ kosikake \\ to + o \left\{ \begin{array}{l} ake \\ sime \end{array} \right\} \\ \text{e\textsc{n}}pitu + o + tot \\ ho\textsc{n} + o + mi \end{array} \right\}$$

Except for a few additional minor reductions, this is about as far as we can go by way of restating the data in the form of a set of rules. We have as yet done little more than describe our corpus, and we must begin to predict sentences not in the corpus. Actually, if these initial sentences had not been carefully chosen, we could scarcely have gotten this far without going beyond the given combinations. To extend our data by more general rules we must have some means of checking our guesses: an informant, or a larger body of data in which to search for missing combinations.

The most obvious guess would be to collapse the first two rules of G_3:

$$S \rightarrow \left\{ \begin{array}{l} doozo \\ watakusi + wa \end{array} \right\} X + te \left\{ \begin{array}{l} kudasai \\ imasu \end{array} \right\}$$

Now we have predicted that *doozo tatte imasu* and *watakusi wa tatte kudasai*, and so on, are Japanese sentences. In this case, our source tells us that they are not, and we must reject the rule.

Next, we turn our attention to the internal make-up of the constituent X. Three items occur before the form o. We hypothesize that they are members of the same class — call it Z. Four items occur after the same form o, and we set up another class W. Finally, we gather together the remaining forms as a class Y. Incorporating these guesses into our description, we restate Rule 3 as a series of rules:

$$3a. \quad X \rightarrow \left\{ \begin{array}{l} Y \\ Z + o + W \end{array} \right\}$$

3b. $Y \rightarrow tat, arui, kosikake$

3c. $Z \rightarrow$ *to, eɴpitu, hoɴ*
3d. $W \rightarrow$ *ake, sime, tot, mi*

Again, we must test our generalizations by trying out the sequences which were not in the original data, for instance:

15. watakusi wa hoɴ o akete imasu
16. watakusi wa hoɴ o simete imasu
17. watakusi wa to o mite imasu
18. watakusi wa eɴpitu o mite imasu
19. watakusi wa to o totte imasu
20. watakusi wa eɴpitu o akete imasu
21. watakusi wa eɴpitu o simete imasu

The new Sentences 15 through 18 are accepted with no question. There is a slight hesitation on 19 (which we note as an important datum in the testing of our theory), but the informant accepts it also. On hearing 20 and 21, the informant is puzzled, and then says that they are all right but "you just wouldn't say that" or that they are nonsensical or the like. We refine our analysis by distinguishing between two subtypes in the class Z: those which can and those which cannot occur (in fully acceptable sentences) with all members of W, and we make a corresponding subdivision in the class W.

Our grammar is thus simplified every time we are able to gather several items into a single class. This operation is symbolized either by putting the items together within braces (as in G_2 above), or by setting up an intermediate element which is developed further in a disjunctive rule (such as X, Y, Z, W in the restatement of G_3 above). Two factors enter into the decision about which of these courses to follow. The first is the length of the list of items gathered into a class: Rules 3b, 3c, and 3d above appear to be essentially lexical lists, and we can expect many additions to these classes as the analysis is extended. This consideration is a more or less practical matter. Of more fundamental importance is the second consideration. That is, can we use an additional node in the P markers posited by the rules? Thus, the representations of Sentence 5 according to the two analyses above (G_2 and G_3 with the later revisions of 3a, and so forth) would be as follows:

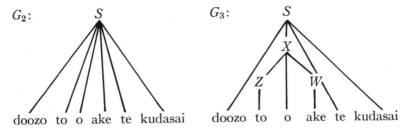

And again, if we break down Z into two subclasses by a rule

$$Z \to \begin{Bmatrix} Z_1 \\ Z_2 \end{Bmatrix}$$

rather than put those two subclasses directly into Rule 3a, we will be building subbranches of the form

$$\begin{array}{c} Z \\ | \\ Z_1 \end{array}$$

into our P markers. If we take this course, we can refer to all members of the subclasses by a general symbol Z in a transformational rule. Clearly, the number of times we need to refer to this class in T rules will be a deciding factor. More important, we can perform manipulations below this node and allow for transformed structures to be attached to Z.

Classes Y and Z both occur before the same items in our sentences. If we could collapse them into a single class, our analysis would be simplified. We can do this by deleting Y from Rule 3a, deleting Rule 3b, and adding the items to Rule 3d. This possibility must be rejected, however, when our informant rejects such strings as *doozo hoN o aruite kudasai.*

So far we have modified the grammar by repeatedly setting up tentative classes on the basis of mutual substitutibility. We may produce further changes by other manipulations, such as deleting items from the original sentences (i.e., substituting null for various parts) and asking whether the new strings are also sentences. By this means we discover eventually that every one of our original (and new) sentences can be matched by one in which *doozo, watakusi wa,* and/or the various members of Z together with *o* are absent. These sentences can be accounted for in two ways. The optionally present items can be set up from the beginning in parentheses. Or we might write deletion transformations to provide for the abbreviated sentences. Taking the first alternative for the time being, we may sum up **the** grammar for this segment of Japanese as follows. (I anticipate further discussion by giving more concrete designations to our classes and constructions, and revise our morphophonemic "spellings" for two items. See Chapter 4, Problem 7.)

G_4:

1. $S \rightarrow \begin{cases} (doozo)\ VP + te + kudasai \\ (watakusi + wa)\ VP + te + imasu \end{cases}$

2. $VP \rightarrow \begin{cases} Verb_i \\ (Noun + o)\ Verb_t \end{cases}$ *i: intransitive*   *t: transitive*

3. $Noun \rightarrow \begin{cases} Noun_1 \\ Noun_2 \end{cases}$

4. $Verb_t \rightarrow Verb_{t1}$ in $Noun_1 + o + \underline{\quad}$

5. $Verb_t \rightarrow \begin{cases} Verb_{t1} \\ Verb_{t2} \end{cases}$

6. $Noun_1 \rightarrow eNpitu$ *pencil*

7. $Noun_2 \rightarrow to,\ hoN$ *door, book*

8. $Verb_{t1} \rightarrow mi,\ tor$ *see, take*

9. $Verb_{t2} \rightarrow ake,\ sime$ *open, shut*

10. $Verb_i \rightarrow aruk,\ tat,\ kosikake$ *walk, stand up, sit down*

Here are the meanings of the other forms: *doozo* means 'please'; *te + kudasai* is a polite imperative construction (*te* is the gerund or nonfinal suffix); *watakusi* means 'I' (polite); *te + imasu* is a polite progressive construction meaning 'I am opening the door,' and so on; *wa* is the topic marker; *o* is the object marker.

I have purposely deferred giving glosses in order to show that a set of rules can be postulated by using the familiar techniques of linguistic analysis: trying out new combinations, attempting to delete items, shifting the items into a new order (although we have not yet tried this with our Japanese sentences), and so on. To know the meanings of the forms is in no way necessary, although it will probably help in setting up crucial tests and conceptualizing our theory. From the meaning — i.e., glosses — we might guess that the sequence that would be rendered in English as 'Please walk the book' is not a sentence, but we cannot be sure before we try it out. The verb in question might mean 'move' in this context, for example. What is necessary, of course, is a source which will tell us which sentences are acceptable and which sequences are not. This is merely to say that linguistics is an empirical science. As such it shares the tentative nature of any science.

The fact that it is often difficult to discover whether or not a given sequence is grammatical and that there remains a large area of indeterminacy is simply a reflection of the subject matter of linguistics. As a cultural institution language is subject to the vagaries of the all-too-human. Any grammatical description (not just a generative grammar) must abstract and select from the intricate realities of geographical and historical variation and from the existence of social dialects and individual quirks.

5.2   Revisions

Let us return to our Japanese example. In the following discussion I shall assume that we have some source for further knowledge about the language and show in what way the rules given above would be modified in a fuller grammar (for a treatment of some of these problems see Richard E. Smith, 1962).

First let us consider the problem of items which may or may not be present, such as the topic (marked by *wa*) and other noun phrases in Japanese sentences. Within the very narrow limits of the data we have considered, it is easiest to account for these items as was done above, that is, by treating them as optionally present items in the PS rules. In a larger context, however, such a technique might be undesirable for several reasons.

The most straightforward argument against such an analysis is the — by now familiar — argument from considerations of simplicity. In the light of the whole theory, a simpler analysis results (in this instance) if the noun phrases are set up as obligatory items and then deleted optionally after they are no longer useful. The deletion transformation is an extremely simple one:

$$X + NP + Y \rightarrow X + Y$$

or the like. To add it (and omit the parentheses in the PS rules) brings very little extra complication into the grammar. If we can find at least a few facts that are more easily accounted for if all the nouns are left in, then the decision will be clear. And there are indeed a number of such instances.

One situation is the following. There is in Japanese a postposition *no* denoting (among other things) more or less what is meant by possessive cases or particles like *of* in other languages. Thus, *watakusi no ho*N means 'my book,' *watakusi no tomodati* means 'my friend,' *tomodati no ho*N 'the friend's book,' and so on. Such phrases, which have no upper length limit, are produced by a generalized transformation, the details of which need not concern us here. There are also phrases in which the second or "possessed" noun is not present. These have a pronominal meaning: *watakusi no*, 'my one, mine,' (referring to 'book,' 'friend' and so on). Such phrases also have no length limit: *watakusi no tomodati no ie no*, 'the one of my friend's house.' To account for them in an analysis in which all the noun phrases are optionally selected would be extremely awkward. Moreover, the co-occurrence relationships with verbs are determined by the "understood" noun. For instance, with the exception of some minor types, the concept 'is' (in a certain place), 'exists,' is expressed in Japanese by two verbs: *i* and *ar*. The first occurs with animate, the second with inanimate nouns: *watakusi no wa koko ni iru* 'mine (friend, brother, and so on) is here'; *watakusi no wa koko ni aru* 'mine (book, pencil, and so on) is here.' To account for this possibility, it would be necessary to add a special optional transformation for sentences with a subject ending in *no* to replace *i* by *ar*. The transformation would appear before the regular rule selecting *ar* for inanimate subjects. Or, if this selection is carried out in the PS rules, a series of rules like the following would be necessary (ignoring here the remainder of the strings):

$$Noun + no + \cdots + Verb_x \rightarrow Noun + no + \cdots \begin{Bmatrix} i \\ ar \end{Bmatrix}$$

$$Noun_{an} + \cdots + Verb_x \rightarrow Noun_{an} + \cdots + i$$

$$Verb_x \rightarrow ar$$

On the other hand, if we use an optional deletion transformation, no special rule for phrases ending in *no* is necessary. Similar arguments can be drawn from the complex system of honorific and deferential forms in Japanese.

The second kind of argument for deletion transformations in the treatment of Japanese sentences is no less important but much more tricky to apply. In general, we want our grammar not only to produce the proper strings in the simplest manner, but also to explain the working of the language in a satisfactory way. That is, we ask whether the analysis explains the way certain strings are understood, whether it accounts for the fact that certain strings are ambiguous, and so on (see Section 1.2). Here again, in the Japanese example, the deletion rule provides a natural explanation for the difference in meaning between the two sentences cited in the last paragraph. At the same time, it shows how in Japanese the deletion of noun phrases functions in much the same way that pronominal reference does in other languages, how certain reduced sequences are ambiguous, how certain others are not (with selection of honorific or deferential forms before the deletion of nouns).

The latter arguments are much harder to pin down than the arguments from simplicity. Linguists differ greatly in the weight that they attach to these two — occasionally conflicting — sets of criteria. We may draw two conclusions from the sometimes heated discussions that have arisen over the use of such phrases as "explanatory power" or "the native speaker's intuition about linguistic form." One is that when an analysis simplifies a grammar and at the same time seems to explain the functioning of the language in a better way, then the investigator may feel encouraged that he is on the right track. The other conclusion is that we need to sharpen the concepts of "explaining," "intuition," and so on, and, if possible, devise significant tests to get at these rather elusive notions.

One fairly clear-cut area is that of ambiguity. There will generally be much more agreement among native speakers as to whether a given string is ambiguous (when spoken out of context!) than there will be, say, on the proper analysis of a sentence into immediate constituents. There are at least three different published analyses of the sentence *The King of England opened Parliament.* But there seems to be no disagreement about various examples of ambiguous sentences that have appeared, such as *Flying planes can be dangerous.*

We can state as a general requirement for a total theory of a language that any ambiguous sequence must have several representations in the theory. This requirement is quite parallel to the condition placed on a phonological theory that no two sequences that are "different" (i.e., consistently distinguishable by a pair test) may be represented phonemically in the same way. That is, beyond the phonological level, we can demand that no two sequences that are "different" may be represented in the same way, even if they happen to have the same phonemic shape. Some of these differences will be accounted for by a theory of language usage ("pragmatics" in the sense of Charles Morris, 1938). Some, presumably, will be accounted for by a semantic theory: *Look at the table* is ambiguous only because *table* has several meanings, e.g., 'mathematical table,' 'dinner table.' In the realm of grammar proper, different representations may exist, as we have seen, on the level of phrase structure (different P markers for the same string). They may also exist in the transformational level, as in the example of the last paragraph, or in other often cited sentences such as *I don't approve of his cooking,* or *John is crazy to go.*

Returning to our Japanese sentences, we consider the other

optionally present item, the particle *doozo,* 'please.' This form is of extremely limited distribution. Except for a few minor stereotyped expressions, it occurs only with polite imperative sentences. Again, this optional form could be derived in two ways. If the polite imperative is included in the PS rules, *doozo* could be derived by a context-restricted rule from an optional element that leads to a small class of sentence openers (such as *hai* 'yes,' *iie* 'no'). Or, if the polite imperative is produced by a simple optional T rule (as seems more likely), the form could simply be tacked on to the derived imperative sentence. Since nothing particularly important happens to such a form as *doozo* in the transformational processes of Japanese — in other words, since there is no need to specify an elaborate relationship between *doozo* and the rest of the P markers of sentences in which it occurs — the latter course would seem to be preferable.

Both of the situations we have considered illustrate a frequent alternative which is faced in constructing a transformational grammar: whether to produce some possible construction directly in the PS rules or by means of a T rule. We may elaborate this discussion by considering a similar situation in the grammar of English, namely, the question of producing imperative sentences. We shall consider some of the arguments in favor of an analysis in which imperatives are not produced directly in the PS rules but by means of transformations in which the subject is deleted. First of all, it should be made clear that such a treatment in no way depends on the idea that the subject of an imperative sentence is "really there" or "understood" in the mind of the speaker. Rather, such an analysis can be shown to be preferable merely on grounds of simplicity.

It seems fairly clear that of the following pairs only the sentences in the first column are fully well formed, while those in the second are not, or at least are so peculiar as to provoke reactions of surprise or puzzlement:

1a. Is it true that you are   1b. *Is it true that come?
    coming?

2a. This statement is based   2b. *You are based on error.
on error.

3a. Don't be surprised.   3b. *Don't be based on error.

4a. You are enjoying yourself.   4b. *The statement is enjoying
itself.

5a. ^{2}Enjóy yoursèlf^1 #   5b. *^{2}Enjóy himsèlf^1 #

Sentence 1a is formed in three steps. First, *that* + *S* (where *S* stands for any sentence) is substituted for the article and noun in a sentence of the form $T + Noun_f + Aux + be + Adj$. Then there is an optional switch of position and addition of *it* to yield strings of the form $It + Aux + be + Adj + that + S$, which is finally made into a question. Now if the imperative sentence is derived directly from *S* in PS rules, we must somehow specify that sentences undergoing the first step of this derivation cannot be of the imperative type (to prevent the formation of strings like 1b). In other words, the rules for *that* clauses in sentences like 1a and several other types must be made less general.

The remaining examples suggest that not just any sentence can occur in an imperative form, that it is in fact precisely the sorts of sentences allowing *you* (or animate, perhaps human nouns) as subject that do occur in this subjectless form. If imperatives are produced in the phrase structure, then every restriction on the verbal complexes that can co-occur with such nouns (including selections involving the object for passive sentences) will have to be duplicated for subjectless imperative sentences. Sentence 5a (and its ungrammatical counterpart) show further that it is specifically *you* that must be assumed as subject of the strings underlying imperatives. Finally, the passive example shows that if the passive is derived by transformations, then the imperative will also have to be so derived, unless passives are to be derived by two separate processes, one for imperatives and one for nonimperatives (see Lees and Klima, 1963).

Before leaving our Japanese examples, we may point out one more revision that would be made in a more complete grammar. An examination of more sentences would show that the form *watakusi*,

'I' (polite, compare *boku*, 'I' familiar) differs in no way from what we have called nouns; in a finer set of noun classes the words corresponding to English pronouns are merely members of the class of animate nouns.

5.3   Grammatical Relations

In the remainder of this chapter we shall consider some of the types of grammatical restrictions that are encountered in various languages. We shall then attempt to survey possible ways of accounting for these restrictions in a grammar of rules.

The basic relations that can obtain between the elements of a grammatical theory and the corresponding relations in the language described by the grammar are surprisingly few. The bewildering variety encountered in any real language results from the interplay of these basically simple relations. In the following discussion we may consider some of these possibilities one by one and in each instance start from an ideal abstract system.

★5.4   Relations of Order

The most obvious relations holding between items in a string and in the rules describing them are those of order. That is, any rule yielding more than one element (and there must be such rules or else every sentence will consist of only one form) will specify that the elements are arranged in a definite way:

$$X \to Y + Z$$

The limiting cases here would be languages in which the order of elements is completely fixed and those at the other extreme in which the order is completely free.

The preceding descriptions are rather vague. If we try to restate them more precisely we find several possibilities. Let us call a language a **fixed-order** language if it has the following property: for every pair of terminal elements x and y in the language, if x precedes y in a sentence, then y precedes x in no sentence. Such a language would be, for instance, one with the natural numbers (1, 2, 3, · · ·) or some part of them as terminal elements (not terminal *strings*, of course). Every string of the form $\# X + a + Y + b + Z \#$ (X, Y, Z perhaps null) in which a were greater than b would be ungrammatical. That is, any such language could be described by a grammar in which designations for the terminal elements would be chosen from the natural numbers in such a way that if a always preceded b, a would be designated by a number smaller than the number designating b. If every natural language is an infinite set of strings constructed out of a finite set of elements, then it follows that no natural language is a fixed-order language in this sense. A grammar for such a language would have to follow these restrictions: (1) there would be no optional transformations or morphophonemic rules rearranging elements into a new order; (2) for any rule $X \rightarrow Y + Z$, there would be no strings in the language dominated by Y and Z in which the same elements appeared; (3) there could be no general rules conjoining two arbitrary sentences to form a new sentence.

A somewhat more realistic system would be one in which the various types of phrases were fixed both in relation to each other and internally, but in which it would be possible for the same type of phrase to reoccur at various points (as in the successive expansions $S \rightarrow NP + VP$, $VP \rightarrow V + NP$). Let us call such a language a **fixed-phrase** language. It would have the following property: if there is in the grammar a string containing the substring (terminal or nonterminal) $X + Y$ such that $X + Y$ is dominated by Z, then there is no string in the grammar containing the substring $Y + X$ such that $Y + X$ is dominated by Z. ("In the grammar" means "in the strings generated by the grammar.") Because we have used such expressions as "type of phrase" (indeed, "phrase" itself), this description refers not just to a language as a set of strings but as a language described by a particular grammar. Such a system seems to be equivalent to the theory of language structure posited by tagmemic descriptions in which there are no "process statements" (i.e., usually implicit transformations) describing one arrangement of items in terms of another. It is also the system of the PS terminal "languages" described by the PS component of most transformational grammars. Such a system would again have no optional permutations.

Still another variation might be called a **semi-fixed** language. In such a language if there is a sentence $\# a + b + c + d \#$, then there are no sentences $\# a + c + b + d \#$, $\# a + d + b + c \#$, and so forth. That is, given a set of elements co-occurring in a sentence, these elements can occur in only one order. Such a system is different from a fixed-order language, as can be seen from the example of a language with the strings

$$\begin{matrix} 1 + 2 + 3 \\ 2 + 1 + 4 \end{matrix} \quad \text{but not} \quad \begin{matrix} *1 + 2 + 4 \\ *2 + 1 + 3 \end{matrix}$$

Since no mention is made of the dominating elements, it also differs from a fixed-phrase language.

It is doubtful whether there are any natural languages conforming to any of these types. But most, if not all, languages have subparts of essentially the fixed-phrase type, most commonly in their morphological systems, that is, on the level of word construction. It might appear that in such subparts the order of elements at the higher level of representations would conform to the order of elements in the terminal strings. For instance, in English noun phrases the article (*the, a, some,* and so on) always appears before the noun (if the article is present at all) and any optionally present adjectives. It is clearly simpler to produce this order directly in the rule $NP \rightarrow T + N$ than to produce first the order $N + T$ and then add a rule switching (transformationally) the order of these two elements.

However, it sometimes turns out that a simpler total grammar results if strings are first produced in a nonterminal order and then rearranged by a low-level switch. Such is often the case in dealing with discontinuous constituents, as we have seen in our treatment of Language X (Sections 3.6, 4.5). For example, the combinations of elements making up the auxiliary in English are usually given in something like the following order

$$Aux \rightarrow C(M)(have + en)(be + ing)$$

where C becomes either *Past* or the third-person singular suffix Z_3 or null; M stands for modal (*will, can, may,* and so forth); *en* is the past participle formant; and *Aux* has previously been introduced before the main verb complex. A low-level rule then rearranges the various affixes (*en, ing, C*) and any following verbal base (including *have, be*) into the terminal order. The rule as given is simply an explicit counterpart to the statement that the "perfect," "progressive" and "modal" constructions are independently chosen (with a statement of their internal make-up). There are several other reasons for setting up the elements in the order given. One is the superficially erratic behavior of the auxiliary verb *do;* the verb can be neatly accounted for as a carrier for unattached affixes after the operation of several optional transformations and the obligatory switch mentioned above. Another argument rests on the nominalizing transformations which prefix *ing* to verb phrases in a very general way. To position the *ing* in its terminal order as a suffix to the front verb in the verbal complex would necessitate a very long enumeration of the possible items occurring first in the strings that can undergo the nominalizing T rules.

Finally, as the reader can easily convince himself, to set up the affixes as suffixes from the beginning would necessitate a series of context-restricted rules. In general, of two grammars which generate the same strings, the simpler one (other things being equal) will be that one which has fewer context-restricted rules. This principle often provides a formal method of choice between two competing sets of rules and a formal support for intuitively based decisions. Thus (to take up an example from the beginning of Chapter 3), the analysis of *The man gave me a book* into two parts of three words each, of each of these parts into two parts, and so on (as illustrated below), is counter-intuitive. In addition, if we try to generalize our grammar to produce *John went to the state capital* (conforming to the same structure), we find that the grammar dissolves into a mass of context-restricted rules. Moreover, they will produce only these two sentences, whereas a more reasonable analysis will also generate *John gave me a book, the man went to the state capital,* and others. (This analysis would follow from a theory which stated that all constructions are binary and symmetrical.)

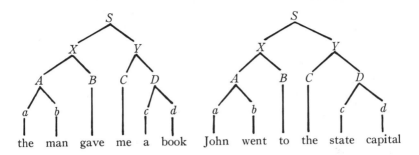

Another situation in which we might depart from a fixed terminal order of items would be the following. Suppose we have a construction in which a large number of items in various positional classes can be freely combined. However, a few special combinations violate the otherwise prevailing arrangements on which we have based our positional classifications. For instance, imagine a construction in which there is one final obligatory item preceded by two optional classes and that the items occur in this order in all instances but one:

$$\left(\begin{Bmatrix} a \\ a' \end{Bmatrix}\right) \left(\begin{Bmatrix} b \\ b' \end{Bmatrix}\right) \begin{Bmatrix} C \\ C' \end{Bmatrix}$$

However, if a' and C occur next to each other, they must occur in the order $C + a'$. We can account for this easily by a single additional T rule $a' + C \rightarrow C + a'$, whereas to produce this order directly would demand a much more intricate set of rules.

Similarly, when we encounter a system which — described in positional terms — has several items which are mutually exclusive with items occurring somewhere else in the construction, we can often simplify by setting up a description in which all the mutually exclusive items occur in the same position. Then by a low-level rearrangement we can adjust the position of the various items. For instance, suppose we have a set of verbal suffixes with third-person

plural mutually exclusive with first- and second-person suffixes but
separated in their position by some other item:

Verb + Tense
Verb + Plural + Tense
Verb + Tense + 1st-sing
Verb + Tense + 1st-plural, etc.

We can describe this system as follows:

$$X \to Verb + Tense \left(\begin{Bmatrix} 1st \\ 2nd \end{Bmatrix} \right) (Plural)$$

Now, after the rules which turn *1st* plus *Plural*, and so forth, into
the proper forms, we add a rule

Tense + Plural → Plural + Tense

to provide for the proper sequence of the second possibility given
above. As this example shows, a rearrangement into a hypothetical
order often suggests other regularizations.

At the opposite pole to the types with more or less fixed order
would be languages with completely free orderings. Here again,
there are various possible situations to consider. Corresponding to
what we have called fixed-order languages would be **free-order**
languages, in which the items in any terminal string could be rearranged in any way, the result still being a sentence of the language.
If we interpret this description literally and take "item" to mean
any segment down to the smallest in the terminal strings, then
such a language could be described by a grammar which ended
with a "shuffling" rule

$$\# X + Y + Z \# \to \# Y + X + Z \#$$

in which X, Y and Z could be understood to range over any string.

Next in respect to the amount of freedom in ordering of items
would be various kinds of **partially free** languages. In such systems,
which are a little easier to imagine than a completely free system,
at least one level of elements would be internally fixed in order but
could be freely ordered with respect to each other. For instance,
there might be a language in which the morphemes could be freely

ordered but the morphemes themselves would be represented by fixed sequences of phonemes. Classical formal Latin is often cited as a language in which the order of words is free while the internal make-up of the words is fixed. The three sequences separated by spaces in the sentence *Puell-am agricol-a ama-t* can presumably be scrambled into any arrangement, but the same is not true of the smaller items. For example, **ampuell agricolt amaa* is not a sentence of Latin. This notion of free word order in Latin is probably closer to the truth for the language of poetry than for prose. Even so, it cannot be considered accurate in full generality. Another possibility would be a language with internally fixed phrasal sequences which could be ordered freely with respect to each other. Modern German and English offer varying degrees of approximation to this type. In both of them there are various types of phrases — prepositional, noun phrases, combinations of adverb plus adjective, and so on — which are internally more or less fixed but which can occur in various places relative to each other.

In all of these types, the differing arrangements could presumably be associated with differences of meaning or not. In the latter case (what Harris, 1951, has called "descriptively equivalent" order) the language would be a language of combinations of items rather than of sequences. In most instances there seems to be at least a difference of emphasis.

PS rules are inherently incapable of generating freely ordered combinations of items in a neat way. Let us construct some languages showing some of the properties of free ordering. In the first (L_1) every permutation of the triple *abc* is a sentence, as is every permutation of the triples $a'b'c'$, $a''b''c''$. That is, the strings *abc, acb, bca, bac*; $a'b'c'$, $b'c'a'$, and so forth, are sentences, but not *aab, b, ab'c, a'bc''*, and so on. A PS grammar with only one pair of braces would simply be a listing of all eighteen possible sentences:

$$S \rightarrow \begin{Bmatrix} abc \\ acb \\ bac \\ bca \\ \text{etc.} \end{Bmatrix}$$

In terms of the number of symbols, this will not be a very simple grammar. That is, even though we have only nine terminal symbols, our grammar will have 55 symbols. We can reduce this number by using inner braces (to 46), but this is still a rather unwieldy description. We can describe the same system by the following transformational grammar (among others):

Given: $\# S \#$

1. $S \to XXX$

2. $\# X \to \# \begin{Bmatrix} a \\ a' \\ a'' \end{Bmatrix}$

3. $\begin{bmatrix} a \\ a' \\ a'' \end{bmatrix} X \to \begin{bmatrix} ab \\ a'b' \\ a''b'' \end{bmatrix}$

4. $\begin{bmatrix} b \\ b' \\ b'' \end{bmatrix} X \to \begin{bmatrix} bc \\ b'c' \\ b''c'' \end{bmatrix}$

T. Optional: $\# YXZ \# \to \# XYZ \#$

Since Y and Z (as usual) include the possibility of null, the transformation will have the desired effect of producing all permutations of the terminal elements (which are defined as X's in the PS rules). It is easy to see that a more realistic and intricate set of grammatical strings would entail a vastly more complex series of PS rules if all permutations (or a sizable part of them) had to be listed. The number of permutations of n items is $n!$; that is n factorial $= n(n-1)(n-2) \cdots (n-n+1)$. For example, for $n = 10$, $n! = 3,628,800$. With the use of braces to collapse similar rules, the number of symbols necessary to describe all permutations of 10 items directly would be 9,864,100. This last figure is obtained by summing n, $n \cdot (n-1)$, $n \cdot (n-1) \cdot (n-2)$, and so forth, down to $n!$.

L_1 is a free-order language in the sense defined. L_2, which can be derived from L_1 if a, b, c, a', and so forth, are not terminal

symbols but symbols for classes of words, would be a language of
the partially free type with words as the shiftable units (like the
popular idea of classical Latin). The generality of the T rule given
above depends on the fact that each of the terminal elements is
derived from a general symbol X and this specification depends
in turn on a series of context-restricted rules. Let us consider a new
language (L_3) which comes a little closer to a natural language.
L_3 consists of freely ordered strings of words of the following types:
connective sentences with two nouns in the nominative case and
a copulative verb; transitive sentences with two nouns, one in the
nominative and the other in the accusative, and a transitive verb;
intransitive sentences with one noun in the nominative and an
intransitive verb. Even in such a system, to derive all the words
from a single symbol such as was done with L_1 requires a rather
intricate set of rules:

Given: $\# S \#$

1. $S \rightarrow X + X(X)$
2. $X + X + X \rightarrow X \begin{Bmatrix} Verb_{cop} \\ Verb_{tr} \end{Bmatrix} X$
3. $Verb_{tr} + X \rightarrow Verb_{tr} + Noun + Acc$
4. $X + X \rightarrow X + Verb_{intr}$
5. $X \rightarrow Noun + Nom$
6. $Noun \rightarrow puer, puell, \cdots$ etc.

In other words, one has to produce all the various lengths of strings
of X's and then produce the various restrictions by context-
restricted rules. In a more realistic system such as "mythical Latin"
with the additional possibilities of gender and number selections,
numerous optional elements, negatives, several other cases, and a
complex set of verbal inflections, such a description would be
unimaginably complicated. There are two ways to avoid this difficulty. One is to make several special transformations in which the
actual word types are specified: one for nouns, one for verbs, and
so on. The alternative approach takes advantage of the possibility

to set up various boundary symbols. For instance, in describing the language L_3 (without the derivation of all words from X), we might write a rule replacing $+$ by null (or some other boundary marker such as $-$) before the cases *Nom* and *Acc*, and then state a general shift rule by means of a specially defined variable:

Let $W =$ any string not containing $+$
T. optional: $\# Z + W + Y \# \rightarrow \# W + Z + Y \#$

Such a technique, in effect, identifies by boundary a unit of fixed order and allows the rearrangement of such units. If the list of suffixes were very long, the same result could be obtained by representing each suffix by a string of morphophonemes with a special boundary symbol such as a hyphen prefixed. Then the internal boundary rule could be very simply stated as

$$+ \ \& - \rightarrow - \qquad \text{or} \qquad X + - Y \rightarrow XY$$

Similarly, for partially free languages with a level of shiftable phrases, a special phrase-boundary marker such as / can be entered in appropriate places by PS rules, special conventions with regard to variable symbols can be stated, and rules like the shift transformation above can be used. Here we are marking the external joints of the shiftable units; in the previous example we marked the internal joints.

In all of these various possible systems the problem facing the linguist is to discover the parts of an utterance within which it is possible to say that one item must precede another, and so on. We cannot flatly state that in English the article must precede the noun. When we make such a statement we are tacitly qualifying it to mean an article and a noun in one (minimal) noun phrase. *I gave the man a book* is a perfectly good sentence, in which one noun precedes an article. Similarly, in Japanese it is only with various qualifications that we can say the noun phrases, adverbs, and so on, must precede the verb. To make these qualifications explicit is to construct a grammar of Japanese.

★5.5 Relations of Contiguity

The next set of relations to be considered are those of juxtaposition or **contiguity**. They are closely related to the order relations that we have just considered. That is, we can define such notions as "standing next to" by means of such notions as "precedes." If X precedes Y and there is no (non-null) Z such that X precedes Z and Z precedes Y, then and only then is it the case that X immediately precedes Y. Now we can say that X stands next to Y if and only if either X immediately precedes Y or Y immediately precedes X. Here again, there are various possible situations with respect to this relation (which is symbolized along with the order relation by the concatenation operator $+$).

Let us call a language **compact** if it has the following property: for every two elements x and y that stand next to each other in a string of the language, there is no string in the language in which x and y occur and do not stand next to each other. Every compact language in which the strings consist of more than two different elements is a fixed-order language (although the converse does not hold). Hence (see Section 5.4) it seems reasonable to state that no natural languages are compact languages in this strict sense. The rules for a compact language could include none of the form $X \to W(Y)Z$ nor any optional transformations inserting items between two juxtaposed forms (like the English adjective rules). Similarly, there would be no optional permutational rules (although there might be obligatory ones), again with the proviso that the strings consisted of three or more elements.

Parallel to the fixed-phrase languages discussed above would be **compact-phrase** languages, in which sentences consisted of sequences of strings which were compact internally but which were separated by boundaries across which the restrictions of compactness did not hold. The compact strings would be introduced by rules (or chains of rules) of the form $X \to Y + Z$, or $X \to Y(Z(W))$. There could be no rules generating the compact strings in which the order of selection for optional items were mixed or changed as in the series $X \rightarrow T(S)$, $S \rightarrow (W)U$, or in the single rule $X \rightarrow Y((Z)W)$.

Again, although it seems unlikely that there are natural languages of either of these types throughout their whole grammar, there are parts that conform to these restrictions. And once again it is most commonly the morphological constructions that are of the compact type. If one looks for rules producing compact (and fixed-order) strings, one finds them pre-eminently in the lexical rules and in the rules which introduce the actual minimal terminal elements or symbols for morphemes. The exceptions to this statement turn out to be more-or-less haphazard situations that do not enter into the description at all. For instance, it is only by chance that /hor/, /hors/, and /hórəs/ are all nouns in English. Even if they belonged to the same subclass, we would certainly not introduce them by a lexical rule

$$Noun_x \rightarrow \text{mæn, dag, hór((ə)s)}, \cdots$$

Where we deal with discontinuous morphemes such as the consonantal roots and vocalic affixes of Semitic languages, it is only at the lowest levels that the noncompact nature of the morphemes appears. For instance, we might introduce a form lexically as /k-t-b/ and then derive forms in which two consonants are juxtaposed by using a zero symbol for one of the vowels, in order to make the rules for intertwining consonants and vowels more general.

Precisely because the morphological systems of most languages are systems of relatively fixed, relatively compact constructions with no recursion and hence a finite output, we must expect to find fundamentally different problems and processes when we deal with sentence length constructions.

★5.6   Co-Occurrence Relations

Let us consider next various relations holding between items in strings which we may designate by the cover term of **co-occurrence** (or selectional) relations. This term is generally used in a restricted sense to apply to relations of mutual tolerance holding between classes of bases such as animate nouns, verbs demanding an animate subject, and so on. But much more generally, we can consider all such relations of dependency between items in a string as relations of co-occurrence. For instance, whenever the presence of one item demands or excludes the presence of another, we are dealing with such a relation. Any such restrictions — including such situations as government and concord — are fundamentally of the same type.

All the relations of co-occurrence may be analyzed as variations of the relations that may hold between statements of the form "X is a segment of S_1" and "Y is a segment of S_1" where S_1 in both cases stands for the same string and where X and Y are distinct and neither is included in the other. Further possibilities arise if we add references to the structural analyses of the strings.

If X is a segment of S_1 and Y is a (distinct) segment of S_1, we say that X and Y **co-occur** in S_1. If the statement that X is a segment of S_1 implies that Y is also a segment of S_1, we say that X **requires** Y (i.e., if any string contains X but not Y it is ungrammatical). If X requires Y and Y requires X, we say that X and Y require each other or are **mutually dependent**. Finally, when X and Y never co-occur — that is, if "X is a segment of S_1" implies "Y is not a segment of S_1" (and hence if Y is a segment of S_1, then X is not) — we say that X and Y are **mutually exclusive.**

In order to explicate such notions as concord and government, we need to distinguish between bases and inflections or affixes. In more general terms, we need to distinguish between lexical items and grammatical items. It is difficult (perhaps hopeless) to try to give a description of this distinction that will cover all examples. Roughly speaking, the lexical elements will occur in late rules of the form $X \to \{a, b, c, d, \cdots\}$ (i.e., disjunctive rules giving usually fairly long lists of terminal items). Grammatical items will be introduced as terminal items in various contexts, or as nonterminal items that will be replaced by terminal items in obligatory transformations or morphophonemic rules. Grammatical items may also be introduced in transformational rules. Usually, if E is the environment of a grammatical item y, E will require y or one of a small number of possible replacements for y. But if y is a lexical item, the number of possible replacements for y will be large. The distinction rests ultimately on the grammar postulated for a given language.

Let us consider a simple language, L_4, of two-word sentences each consisting of a noun and a verb, every noun having a plural or singular suffix, every verb also having a number suffix that agrees with the number of the noun. The obvious grammar for L_4 would be something like this:

1. $S \rightarrow N + V$
2. $N \rightarrow Noun \begin{Bmatrix} Sg \\ Pl \end{Bmatrix}$
3. $Sg + V \rightarrow Sg + Verb + Sg_v$
4. $V \rightarrow Verb + Pl_v$
5. $Noun \rightarrow \{n_1, n_2, n_3, \cdots, n_{500}\}$
6. $Verb \rightarrow \{v_1, v_2, v_3, \cdots, v_{200}\}$

According to this grammar, the lexical items would be the nouns and verbs, the number morphemes would be the grammatical items. But it would be possible to describe the language the other way around:

1. $S \rightarrow \begin{Bmatrix} N_1 + V_1 \\ N_2 + V_2 \end{Bmatrix}$
2. $N_1 \rightarrow \{n_1, n_2, n_3, \cdots, n_{500}\} No_1$
3. $N_2 \rightarrow \{n_1, n_2, n_3, \cdots, n_{500}\} No_2$
4. $V_1 \rightarrow \{v_1, v_2, v_3, \cdots, v_{200}\} No_{v1}$
5. $V_2 \rightarrow \{v_1, v_2, v_3, \cdots, v_{200}\} No_{v2}$
6. $No_1 \rightarrow Sg$
7. $No_2 \rightarrow Pl$
8. $No_{v1} \rightarrow Sg_v$
9. $No_{v2} \rightarrow Pl_v$

According to this clearly absurd grammar, the noun and verb stems are the grammatical items and the suffixes are the lexical items (which happen to belong to single-membered classes). In other words, we may describe the distinction between lexical and grammatical items as above, but we must add "with respect to the simplest grammar." There will be many intermediate cases that will not be as clear-cut as the situation in L_4 (for example, prepositions in English). In the following discussion I shall assume that it is possible to distinguish between lexical and grammatical items.

The various relations of co-occurrence outlined above (and there are others) can be treated in various ways. First of all, we may note that there is a direct correspondence between each of three types of rules and three of those relations. A language in which b requires the presence of a might have a rule: $X \rightarrow a(b)$. One in which a and b were mutually dependent might have a rule: $Y \rightarrow a + b$. Finally, a language in which a and b were mutually exclusive might introduce them by a rule:

$$X \rightarrow \begin{Bmatrix} a \\ b \end{Bmatrix}$$

In order to ensure that these restrictions appear in the terminal strings, however, various other stipulations must be made. For instance, in the first case mentioned (b requires a) there must be no other rules introducing b independently into a string. A similar restriction must be made for the second instance.

Generally speaking, we will be faced not with co-occurrences of individual terminal items, but with restrictions in which at least one of the items is nonterminal. A grammar will operate insofar as possible with classes rather than individual items. In L_1 above (Section 5.4) the a's, b's, and c's and the corresponding primes and double primes are mutually exclusive. In L_2 (with the symbols interpreted as symbols for classes) the same statement holds with respect to the classes of items derived from each of these symbols. If we replace the diacritic marks by new symbols (i.e., a' by $a + x$, a'' by $a + y$), then we will have a model for a system of concord. **Government** may be described as a system in which a class of lexical items (bases) requires a class of grammatical items (not directly attached to the governing bases). **Concord** (or agreement) may be described as a system in which two or more sets of grammatical items (e.g., inflections) attached to different lexical items or constructions are mutually dependent (given certain conditions).

The attempt to state such relations explicitly and with the necessary qualifications as to the domain of such restrictions leads to the postulation of a basic set of kernel sentences. More complex sentences can be derived from kernel sentences by optional transformations. Apparently simple statements about government and concord often conceal highly complex situations usually transformational in their implications. Thus, we read in a grammar of German that the preposition *mit* "takes" the dative case. Actually the notion "dative case" (for a language like German) is a highly abstract construct. Translated into explicit terms, this construct means that when we have a string with a segment that has been derived from *mit* + *NP* the *NP* will take various forms depending on whether it becomes a pronoun, a noun phrase of various possible types, and so on, as illustrated (with the various segments, including ø, required by *mit* — given the other items — underlined):

mit mi<u>r</u>
mit di<u>r</u>
mit d<u>em</u> Mann<u>ø</u>
mit d<u>er</u> Frau
mit d<u>em</u> Junge<u>n</u>
mit d<u>en</u> Männer<u>n</u>
mit d<u>er</u> alte<u>n</u> Frau
mit des Vaters gute<u>m</u> Wille<u>n</u>
mit d<u>enen</u> · · · etc.

To treat such situations we set up an item — say *Dat* — which in combination with various other items — some equally abstract — will lead to the proper choices of inflections.

The two grammars given above for L_1 (Section 5.4) indicate two basic techniques for preserving co-occurrence restrictions through PS rules: by directly producing the permitted combinations or by applying context-restricted rules. Many of the problems given in previous chapters have illustrated these techniques. In systems of government and concord a further possibility suggests itself, namely, to produce the proper inflections by obligatory transformations. Let us consider another invented language (reminiscent of the Bantu languages). In L_5 sentences consist (in this order) of a subject noun phrase, an object noun phrase (with transitive verbs) and a verb (transitive or intransitive). The noun phrases consist of an optional and indefinitely long string of adjectives and a noun. Nouns belong to one of three different classes, each with a different prefix, which can itself indicate singular or plural. Adjectives agree in number and (gender) class with the modified noun and take corresponding (singular or plural) prefixes. Finally, the verb contains (in this order) a base, a subject marker selected by the gender and number of the subject noun, and (for transitives) an object marker similarly selected. This language could be described by PS rules of the following sort:

Given: $\# S \#$

1. $S \rightarrow NP \begin{Bmatrix} Verb_{in} \\ NP + Verb_{tr} \end{Bmatrix}$

SPr_1: *singular prefix*
Class 1, and so on.
SSM_1 *means singular*
subject marker for
Class 1 subject, and so on.

2. $NP \rightarrow (Adj) \begin{Bmatrix} \begin{Bmatrix} SPr_1 \\ PPr_1 \end{Bmatrix} Noun_1 \\ \begin{Bmatrix} SPr_2 \\ PPr_2 \end{Bmatrix} Noun_2 \\ \begin{Bmatrix} SPr_3 \\ PPr_3 \end{Bmatrix} Noun_3 \end{Bmatrix}$

3. $Verb_{in} \rightarrow Verb_{intr} \begin{bmatrix} SSM_1 \\ PSM_1 \\ SSM_2 \\ PSM_2 \\ SSM_3 \\ PSM_3 \end{bmatrix}$ in $\begin{bmatrix} SPr_1 \\ PPr_1 \\ SPr_2 \\ PPr_2 \\ SPr_3 \\ PPr_3 \end{bmatrix} \begin{Bmatrix} Noun_1 \\ Noun_2 \\ Noun_3 \end{Bmatrix} —$

Similar (and more complex) rules would continue the selection of subject markers and object markers for transitive verbs. A recursive series of rules might add an indefinite number of adjectives (from *Adj*) again followed by context-restricted rules for concord. It is apparent that the grammar can be simplified considerably if at

least some of these selections are brought about by transformations.

A language with a structure of selectional relations similar to
those of L_5 but with the possibility of rearrangements into any
order cannot be described with PS rules alone under the restrictions
we have adopted. (See Section 3.2.) For if the prefixes and suffixes
are chosen independently, there will be ungrammatical productions;
but if the selections are made by context-restricted rules, there will
be no upper limit to the possible contexts in which a particular
selection must be made. Further, a simpler grammar will result if
the obligatory T rules for concord are placed before the optional
rearrangements.

It should be apparent from the discussion of the last few sections
that the general principle of analysis is to set up a regularized
system which can be easily described and which can then be transformed into the shape of terminal strings. We describe a free-order
language as if it were fixed and then rearrange items. We set up
theoretical constructs to account for the categories that are perti-
nent in systems of government and concord and then coalesce them
into the actual items. We set up terminally discontinuous constructions as continuous ones and then separate them. The method
parallels very closely the method of morphophonemic description,
of which it has been said that it sets up for a language "a fictitious
agglutinating analog, such that a one-way transformation from the
analog to the actual utterance is possible" (Lounsbury, 1953; in
Joos, 1958, p. 380).

Beyond the relations that we have considered in this chapter
there are relations holding between items at different points in the
structure of grammatical representations (such as "dominates,"
"is derived from" and so on). Restrictions on combinations of items
must sometimes be stated in terms of such underlying relations.
For instance, the typical conjunction rules of languages like English
require a reference to the dominating nodes for the conjoined items.
We say *He went home and hurried up the front steps* but not *They
bought a new and are hurrying home* (from *They bought a new home*
and *They are hurrying home*). Similarly, we can modify a noun by

attaching a rearranged sentence originally containing a repetition of the same noun. But we cannot do this if the noun is already contained in (is "part of") a noun phrase in the second sentence: *Give me the package that the book that is in is mine* (from *Give me the package* and *The book that is in the package is mine*. Compare *Give me the package that the book that is mine is in*, see Chomsky, 1962b).

Problems for Chapter 5

1. Extend and modify the grammar of Japanese given in Section 5.1 to account for the following additional data. List some sentences predicted by your rules which are not in the corpus. You may wish to compare Problem 7, Chapter 4, for some of the forms.

anata wa tatte imasu ka   *are you standing up?* (polite)
tatte imasita ka   *were (you) standing up?* (polite)
tatta ka   *did he (you) stand up?* (plain)
hoN o mita   *he (I, you) saw the book* (plain)
anata wa eNpitu o totta ka   *did you take the pencil?* (plain)
watakusi wa arukimasu   *I walk* (polite)
watakusi wa aruku   *I walk* (plain)
aruita ka   *did (he, you) walk?* (plain)
tatte imasu yo   *I am (he is, you **are**) standing up* (polite)
to o akemasu   *he (I, you) opens the door* (polite)
hoN o mimasita   *I (you, he) saw the book* (polite)
watakusi wa kosikakete iru   *I am sitting down* (plain)
aruite ita ka   *were you (was he) walking?* (plain)
to o simete kudasaimasita   *you (he) closed the door* (exalted)
to o sime   *shut the door* (impolite)
hoN o mi yo   *look at the book!* (impolite)
kosikake   *sit down* (impolite)
hoN o mite aruite imasu   *he* (and so on) *is looking at the book as he walks* (polite)
watakusi wa hoN o mite to o simete kosikakemasita   *I looked at the book, closed the door and sat down* (polite)
anata wa to o simete kara hoN o mimasita‾ka   *did you look at the book after you closed the door?* (polite)
to o simete kara kosikakete kudasai   *(please) sit down after you have closed the door* (polite)
tatte kara aruita   *after getting up (I) walked* (plain)
watakusi o mimasita   *(he) saw me* (polite)

2. How would you explain the ambiguities in the following English sentences?

> The committee's appointment was a surprise.
> I just can't see flying kites.
> John feels cold.
> He's crazy to go to Cuba.
> They were ordered to stop picketing.
> Murphy is the one to watch.
> He told me to go without any hesitation.
> She said she was going home today.
> The Danes like good food as well as Americans.
> That's the story of the year.
> On top of everything there was a tarpaulin.
> It's too hot to eat.

3. Write a grammar for the following Russian sentences. Again indicate projections beyond the immediately given corpus.

> júr'ij vráč   *George is a doctor*
> júr'ij búd'it vračóm   *George will be a doctor*
> júr'ij bíl vračóm   *George was a doctor*
> máša vráč   *Mary is a doctor*
> máša búd'it vračóm   *Mary will be a doctor*
> máša bilá vračóm   *Mary was a doctor*
> mój tavár'išč vráč   *my friend is a doctor*
> majá s'istrá bilá vračóm   *my sister was a doctor*
> mají tavár'išči vračí   *my friends are doctors*
> mají tavár'išči búdut vračám'i   *my friends will be doctors*
> mají tavár'išči bíl'i vračám'i   *my friends were doctors*
> máša i júr'ij búdut vračám'i   *Mary and George will be doctors*
> mají s'óstri bíl'i vračám'i   *my sisters were doctors*

4. Write a grammar for the following Finnish sentences. You may wish to compare Problem 9, Chapter 2, for some of the forms.

> myyn talon   *I sell the house*
> myyt talon   *you sell the house*
> en myy taloa   *I am not selling the house*
> et myy taloa   *you are not selling the house*
> myyn talot   *I sell the houses*
> myyt taloja   *you are selling (some) houses*
> en myy taloja   *I am not selling (the) houses*
> myyn taloa   *I am selling the house (and am not through selling it)*
> myy talo   *sell the house!*
> myy talot   *sell (the) houses*

The following are ungrammatical:

>*en myy talon
>*et myy talot
>*myy talon
>*myyn talojen
>*myyt talo

5. Write a series of partly context-restricted rules for the English verbal auxiliary phrases discussed in Section 5.4 — i.e., *will have gone, will be going, goes, can have gone*, and so on — in which the items are arranged in terminal order from the outset.

6. Write the PS grammar implied by the P markers given above (p. 107) for *The man gave me a book* and *John went to the state capital*.

7. Complete the PS rules for L_5 (Section 5.6).

8. Restate the grammar for L_5 by providing for the selection of prefixes and suffixes by obligatory T rules:

   a) In such a way that there are nodes labeled *Pre*, *SM*, and *OM* in the P markers and that these nodes are maintained up to the operation of the obligatory transformations.
   b) In such a way that the nodes of a) above are preserved past the operation of the obligatory transformations.
   c) In such a way that there are no such nodes in the P markers specified by the PS rules (here care must be taken that the T rules do not produce unwanted recursions).

9. Add to the rules for L_5 optional transformations providing for every arrangement (permutation) of the words (i.e., nouns, adjectives, verbs). Make any necessary adjustments in the earlier parts of the grammar.

10. Outline the distinctions or rules that would be necessary to disallow the following sentences in a grammar of English:

   a) Our rubber plant passed away last week.
   b) He's going to go yesterday.
   c) Ephraim, who was my roommate's name, was sitting in the dark.
   d) I beckoned to myself to come.
   e) The mouse ate a wheat.
   f) They are to arrive in the 20th of July on 1963.
   g) His having of a Cadillac irritated me.
   h) Wood is consisted of by this table.
   i) What is he looking out the window that faces?
      (Answer: He is looking out the window that faces the garden.)
   j) This is the cat that the meal was eaten by the rat that was killed by.

CHAPTER SIX

THE PHONOLOGICAL COMPONENT

6.1   From Symbol to Sound

Assuming that a grammatical theory will have at least the parts
we have so far discussed — a set of string-replacement rules
obeying the restrictions of PS rules, and a set of obligatory and
optional transformational rules of a more complex sort — we now
turn our attention to the final component or components necessary
to complete the grammar. The product of the first two sets of rules
— what might be called the "syntactic" rules — will be a set of
T terminal strings each with an associated set of representations:
a final derived P marker for the terminal string, a record of the
T rules which it has undergone and the order of their application,
and the P markers for all the underlying PS terminal strings which
have gone into its composition. Given some or all of this information, our final rules must specify the phonological shape of each T
terminal string.

There are several possibilities for the phonological component
of a transformational grammar. We shall outline a few of them. To
discuss these alternatives in full detail would go well beyond the
limits of this introduction. For more elaborate presentations,

the reader will be referred to several works listed in the bibliography.

Underlying any phonological theory for a specific language,
however, no matter how conceived, we must assume some universal
phonetic theory. Such a theory is implied by a description which
uses such articulatory terms as "velar," "voiced," "implosive,"
and so on. That is, somewhere in specifying the phonetic detail of a
given language we reach a point where the rules for any language
will be the same. In the "super grammar" consisting of the
grammars for all languages, we make a simplification by stating
these lowest level rules only once and referring the output of the
phonetic specifications for any given language to this universal
set of rules. Such a universal theory is empirical, hence subject to
revision as more languages are investigated. In technical terms it
will be or include a "semantic" theory giving the denotations of
the phonetic symbols in terms of classes of physical events. The
events so designated may be physiological — i.e., articulatory — or
acoustic, ideally both. The advent of the sound spectrograph and
other electronic instruments for the study of sounds has provided
a tremendous impetus to research in general phonetic theory. The
task of relating the physical description of linguistic events to the
facts of articulation, perception, and cultural utilization is far from
complete, but the outlook is encouraging.

6.2   Phonological Rules

Perhaps the most obvious scheme for the phonological component
of a transformational grammar would be the following: the input
for our **phonological rules** (P rules) will be the T terminal strings,
that is, strings of concatenated symbols (**formatives**) and boundary
markers of various kinds, roughly equivalent to morphemic
representations. The P rules will be string-replacement rules which
will turn these morphemic representations into strings of phonetic
symbols defined in some general phonetic theory. Since we no longer

need to provide structural descriptions of the kind yielded by PS rules, we can drop all restrictions on the P rules. They may delete items, rearrange them into a new sequence, change several symbols at a time, and introduce new items (e.g., epenthetic vowels) in certain contexts from null. The rules can be set up in such a way that at a given point we will have representations that may be called phonemic, the remaining rules providing a phonetic description of any desired degree of narrowness. In such a case, the first set of rules will parallel closely what have been called morphophonemic rules (or descriptions) in more traditional treatments — that is, rules which turn strings of morphemes into strings of phonemes (or more precisely, phonemic symbols).

It is clear, however, that a breakdown into morphophonemic and "phonemo-phonetic" rules is introduced only at the cost of extra complication in the grammar. As long as a grammar is viewed as a theory which will specify the grammatical strings in a language, there seems to be no particular reason for setting up a level of representation intermediate between the morphemic and the phonetic levels (see, e.g. Halle, 1959). It should be emphasized that such a division can be made within the framework of a transformational grammar. If there are independent reasons for doing so that seem to override the considerations of economy, then a phonemic level can be easily built in.

I am using here the term "phonemic" in one of the several ways in which it has been used in the last decades, that is, as a system of transcription which is "biunique" in the following sense. For every utterance in the language a transcription is uniquely determined. For every transcription in the system an utterance is uniquely determined. That is to say, two utterances are associated with the same transcription if and only if they are functionally identical. Further, the proper transcription for an utterance does not depend on "understanding" the utterance or on being able to reconstruct its syntactic structure. (Various other conditions must be mentioned, such as the reduction of symbols, but they need not concern us here.) Something like this interpretation is probably still the most widespread view in American linguistics (as reflected in texts like Gleason, 1961).

Two sorts of situations show that a phonemic level (in this sense) introduces an unnecessary complication. In many languages a cluster of consonants must either be all voiced or all voiceless. Occasionally such a limitation applies not only to consonants which have voiced (or voiceless) counterparts as separate phonemes but also to consonants with no such counterparts but with voiced or voiceless allophones. In such situations, the preservation of a phonemic level requires the statement of two exactly parallel rules, one at the level of phoneme substitution, one at the level of allophone selection. For instance, in some varieties of German the voiced velar fricative (or uvular trill) /r/ is represented by an unvoiced allophone before voiceless stops. In all dialects of Standard German, the morphophoneme *z* is represented by /s/ in the same environment. If we think of the morphophonemic rule as a substitution of /s/ for /z/ (i.e., a devoicing of /z/), then, phonetically speaking, precisely the same rule may be used to account for the replacement of [r̥] by [r̥]. However, neither the input to our rule, "raizt, varten," nor the output of our rule, "raist, var̥ten," is a phonemic representation according to the prevailing interpretation of this term. The representation "raizt" is not phonemic since the form it represents (*reist*) is indistinguishable from the form represented by "raist" (*reisst*), and one of the requirements for a biunique phonemic representation is that no "sames" (in terms of a pair test) be represented differently. On the other hand, "var̥ten" is not a phonemic representation, since [r] and [r̥] fulfill all the requirements (complementary distribution, phonetic similarity) for being allophones of the same phoneme.

The other situation has to do with the requirement that "higher-level" information is not needed to specify the phonetic shape of a phonemic representation. This condition precludes the use of such information as the presence of morphological boundaries for choosing the allophones of a phoneme. Here again a well-known situation in German may serve as a case in point. There are in most

varieties of Standard German two phones [ç] and [x]. In monosyllabic utterances they are in complementary distribution, the
latter appearing after /a o u/, the former everywhere else. However, in utterances of more than one syllable (and morpheme)
contrasts occur: [táuçən] 'little rope' versus [táuxən] 'dive,' and
so on. One can save the situation by positing a phoneme of internal
open juncture ("plus-juncture") with rather dubious phonetic
characteristics (lengthening of preceding stressed syllable, and
so on). But in some dialects it seems that pairs such as the above
are truly minimal. In a grammar of rules it is easy to take care of
the situation simply by ordering properly the rules for deletion of
boundary symbols and for choice of [x] and [ç] both from a single
symbol. In a biunique phonemic representation such distinctions
will have to appear in the phonemic inventory as well as the list
of phones, where they will appear in any case (see Moulton, 1947,
and Leopold, 1948, both in Joos, 1958).

According to this view of the phonological component, then, the
final set of rules will be simple unrestricted rules turning morphemic
representations into phonetic ones. The bulk of the rules will be
obligatory. Optional rules will deal only with variant styles of
speech, slightly variant dialects, and so on. The grammar can
again be considerably simplified if the rules are at least partly
ordered. And, again following a principle that we have often
adduced, the grammar will be simplified if all representations of
lexical items, grammatical morphemes, and so on, are represented
from the beginning in as near terminal shape as possible. That is,
rather than using Chinese characters or numbers for our morphemic
representations, we use morphophonemic "spellings" which will
then enter directly into the phonological rules. Stated a little more
precisely, we represent our strings in the lowest level of the
syntactic component — i.e., the T terminal strings — by strings
of symbols. These are then mapped by one-to-one rules (usually
left unstated) into the concatenated symbols (primes) upon which
the first rules of the phonological component operate. For instance,
a final T rule might replace the plus sign by # (at appropriate

places) now standing for word boundary. Then the rules mentioned would reinterpret as primes for the P rules the symbols used in representing forms:

$$\# \, hiy + gow + PAST + howm \, \#$$
$$\# \, hiy \, \# \, gow + PAST \, \# \, howm \, \#$$
$$\# + h + i + y + \# + g + o + w + PAST$$
$$+ \# + h + o + w + m + \#$$

Note that *PAST* is still a prime, which by P rules such as the following will combine with certain strings to produce various forms of the past tense:

$$\# + g + o + w + PAST \rightarrow \# + w + e + n + t$$

The P rules will operate to select the proper morph shapes and allophones. The examples of Section 2.4 (in part) illustrate these two sorts of rules. Besides the phonologically determined choices of allomorphs (automatic alternation), it is often convenient to provide special symbols in the morphophonemic representations which will, in effect, extend the automatic alternations to include these morphophonemically conditioned choices.

In German, for instance, along with the large bulk of regular ("weak") verbs that form their past and participial forms according to phonemically predictable processes, there is a group of so-called strong verbs (numbering about two hundred stems) with unpredictable forms. These irregular formations can be taken care of by special rules for the individual verbs (like the special rules for irregular plurals in English nouns). However, when all the forms are accounted for, there will be something like a thousand minimal rules. If we introduce into the morphophonemic representations of these verbs in the lexical rules a special morphophoneme identifying the stems as "strong" and use a special symbol for certain vowel alternations ("umlaut"), the special rules can be cut down to a small fraction of the previous number. In other words, given the information that a verb is irregular (strong), it turns out that significant generalizations about its terminal shape in the past tense, and so on, can be made. The number of special rules referring to particular verbs will be far fewer. Similarly, we might account for the two types of nouns in Language X (Section 3.5) by "spelling" all nouns in one of the classes with a special final morphophoneme, which would then combine with the number suffixes to produce the proper forms.

Besides introducing special morphophonemic symbols for such situations, the morphophonemic representations may depart from traditional phonemic representations in other ways. Let us consider another example from German. In any biunique phonemic analysis of German, three nasal consonants will be distinguished: /m n ŋ/. As in other Germanic languages, the last phoneme — a velar nasal — has an extremely limited distribution, is in complementary distribution with the other two before stops in close transition, and is not represented by a separate symbol in the traditional orthography. Minimal contrasts appear medially as in the pair /zínən/ 'ponder' versus /zíŋən/ 'sing,' in the orthography *sinnen* and *singen*, respectively. In some varieties of German, contrasts also appear finally, as in the past forms of the above verbs /zan/ and /zaŋ/ (but commonly in North German /zaŋk/). If we represent the medial consonant in such forms as *singen* by *ng* — that is, if we strike "ŋ" from the roster of morphophonemes — the rules for strong verb alternations can be considerably simplified. The rule for the past participle of strong verbs with a base ending on a single nasal morphophoneme will give us the correct form for such verbs as *sinnen, spinnen, schwimmen* (with bases represented as "zin, špin, švim") and will not yield the incorrect forms for *singen, schwingen* ("zing, šving"). On the other hand, the rule for past participles ending on nasal plus stop symbols (*schinden, sinken,* and so forth) will also apply to verbs like *singen* to give the correct forms *geschunden, gesunken* and also *gesungen* (cf. *geschwommen*). The phonetic (or phonemic) facts can then be accounted for by a rule replacing "n" by "ŋ" before velar stops. Finally, the dropping of "g" in various environments can be predicted. As an extra support for this analysis, we can account for the common North German pronunciation of word final /ŋ/ as /ŋk/ simply by optionally deleting one of the environments for the dropping of "g." Then the North German pronunciation will result automatically from the general devoicing rule for word final obstruents.

A word of warning is in order here. Rules of the sort we have been considering have been called both phonological rules and morphophonemic rules (also morphonetic). In some presentations of transformational rules (see Lees, 1960) the word "morphophonemic" has been used for certain obligatory rules specifying the morphological shape of various items. However, these rules are still transformational in complexity (i.e., in them information about the P markers of terminal strings is assumed). It is important to remember that the P rules (as we have called them here) differ from T rules in much the same way that PS rules do. However, since every string is dominated by itself, it is possible to carry out essentially simple rewrites by T rules, if it is ever convenient to do so.

6.3   Distinctive Features

The scheme for a phonological component such as the one sketched above has been modified in several directions. In such a system the morphophonemic symbols are treated as single unanalyzed signs. When several members of a class of such signs (e.g., stops, nasals) are referred to, it is necessary in a completely explicit grammar either to define various signs (e.g., "let $C = p, t, k, g, f$," and so on), or to name all members of the class in each rule involving them. In practice, of course, and according to the aims of the particular presentation, such explicitness is often lacking. It is assumed that the reader knows which signs are members of the class of consonant symbols, and so on.

The first departure from this relatively simple scheme comes from beginning not with unanalyzed signs such as p, a, t, and so forth, but rather with sets of phonetic features that give the relevant specifications for the forms of the language. Such specification is needed in any case. The distinctive feature approach differs from the system considered above primarily in the point at which such specification takes place.

In such a scheme, in effect, the lexical rules in the phrase structure are not of the form *Noun → pat* but rather of the following form:

$$
Noun \rightarrow
\begin{vmatrix} bilabial \\ \quad closure \\ \\ velic\ closure \\ \\ fortis \\ open\ glottis \end{vmatrix}
\begin{vmatrix} low\ tongue\ position \\ central\ tongue \\ \quad position \\ lack\ of\ oral \\ \quad obstruction \\ \\ glottis\ in\ voicing \\ \quad position \end{vmatrix}
\begin{vmatrix} alveolar \\ \quad closure \\ \\ velic\ closure \\ \\ fortis \\ open\ glottis \end{vmatrix}
$$

Here the vertical lines enclose "simultaneously present" features. Each such column denotes a particular segment of the form.

The use of features from the beginning has a distinct advantage: the various classes of morphophonemes operated on by various rules can be specified explicitly and neatly merely by naming the features that define them. For instance, in voicing rules (such as the one given for Language X, Section 2.4) in which stops are voiced between vowels, we do not need either to name all the vowels or to define a special symbol by enumerating the symbols for vowels. We can merely write a rule replacing the feature "voiceless" by "voiced" whenever the features shared by the class of stops occur between the features shared by the class of vowels:

$$
\begin{vmatrix} features\ de\text{-} \\ \quad fining\ stops \\ voicelessness \end{vmatrix}
\rightarrow
\begin{vmatrix} features\ de\text{-} \\ \quad fining\ stops \\ voicing \end{vmatrix}
\text{in env.}
\begin{vmatrix} vowel \\ \quad features \end{vmatrix}
-
\begin{vmatrix} vowel \\ \quad features \end{vmatrix}
$$

Or, if the opposition between voiced and voiceless sounds had not yet been specified for stops, the feature of voicing could be simply introduced at this point in the stated environment.

The implementation of the feature approach has not, in actual practice, utilized articulatory features such as the ones shown above, but rather features which are meant to have both articu-

latory and acoustic correlates. Workers in this field — largely
students and associates of Roman Jakobson — have furthermore
attempted to find a small set of binary oppositions that would be
adequate to describe the phonology of any language. The forms of
the language are then represented by matrices of pluses and
minuses. Each column stands for a segment and each row for a
particular feature, its presence in the segment being denoted by
a plus, its absence by a minus. A particular arrangement of the
rows is arrived at for a given language so that the individual signs
are, in effect, not just + or – but "+ in the first row," "– in the
second row," and so on. Since the representation of utterances
by means of sequences of pluses and minuses (and various kinds
of boundaries) makes for great difficulty in following rules,
various alphabetic symbols are still used in presenting the theories.
However, they have no systematic significance and are really
abbreviated statements made for the convenience of the reader.
The fullest explanation of this approach and illustration of its use
in a transformational grammar is found in Halle, 1959 (see also
Halle, 1961, and Halle, 1962). On Jakobsonian phonology — without the application to generative grammars — see also Jakobson
and Halle, 1956, Jakobson, Fant, and Halle, 1952.

6.4   Morpheme-Structure Rules

The second departure from the first type of phonological component described here results from the desire to achieve greater
economy of description by rigorously cutting out all redundant —
that is, predictable — features. On the one hand, this means elimi-
nating the mention of any features that are necessarily present
given the presence of others. An example is the feature of voicing
for all vocalic nonconsonantal segments — i.e., vowels — for languages that have no voiceless vowels. On the other hand, it means
building in the constraints on sequences of sounds by means of a
set of rules called **morpheme-structure** rules. For example, consider
those languages in which clusters of consonants must be either all
voiced or all unvoiced. In giving the phonological shape for any

form (in lexical rules) where such a cluster occurs, we need specify the feature of voicing for only one of the segments. The agreement in this feature can then be carried out by a general rule of morpheme structure. Similarly, in a language in which there is no contrast among nasals occurring immediately before a stop, it is not necessary to specify which nasal occurs in this position, since this information is predictable given the presence of the features defining the class of nasals and the features defining the following stop. The parallel between such incompletely specified segments and the archiphonemes of the Prague school is evident. (See again Halle, 1959.)

The introduction of morpheme-structure rules is attractive, since it provides a natural place in a grammatical theory for important information about the structure of a language, that is, what is often called **phonotactics,** the general statements about permitted sequences of phonemes in short sequences. A transformational grammar without such rules, which represents forms throughout as fully specified sequences of phonemes, will obviously generate only permitted sequences. However, it will offer no information about the possible (but fortuitously nonoccurring) sequences of sounds. For example, it is a general fact of some interest that the sequence [stráyt] is a possible form in English but not in Japanese (even if we make plausible one-for-one substitutions of similar Japanese sounds). The converse is true for the sequence [s·toraito] (with even stress). The addition of morpheme-structure rules makes it possible to account for such facts.

However, the positioning of the morpheme-structure rules presents something of a problem. In structure, these rules clearly belong with the other phonological rules. But since many of the morphological choices must be carried out in the transformational component and depend in some cases on the phonological shape of the lexical items, it would seem that the morpheme-structure rules at least in part must operate before the T rules. This in itself would not be particularly disturbing except for the fact that many forms are introduced only by transformations, e.g., grammatical morphemes, conjunctions, and so on. These transformationally introduced items must themselves obey precisely the same rules of morpheme structure as the lexical items. In other words, the forms introduced by T rules must either be represented as fully specified (at least as far as the redundant features provided by the morpheme-structure rules are concerned), or else we must provide some way to run these newly introduced forms back through the morpheme-structure rules. (See Halle, 1959, pp. 37f.; for an attempt to meet this difficulty, see Bach, 1962b.)

Phonotactic descriptions can be set up apart from the rest of a grammar, in which case we have a set of rules that has been called a "phonological grammar." The rules describing the hypothetical phonemic system of Language X (Section 2.4) offer an example of such a description. In such a case the rules begin with symbols for the longest span over which the constraints apply and continue with the rewriting of these symbols into such symbols as Syllable, Nucleus, Coda, and Consonant (of various types). The rules end with the introduction of the symbols for the various sounds. (For an example of such a phonological grammar for Spanish, see Saporta and Contreras, 1962.) Such a description is of limited interest, however, and remains largely *ad hoc*. That is, the morpheme-structure rules are introduced into a grammar in the interests of economy, form a natural part of a grammatical theory, and *in addition* provide an explanation for the facts of phonotactics. There is no way, on the other hand, in which a set of phonotactic rules (as such) could be fitted into a total grammar.

6.5 Transformational Cycles

The final revision of the phonological component that we shall consider is the introduction of a special set of rules which are concerned merely with specifying the phonological shape of terminal strings but which are still transformational in scope. Such rules have grown out of the attempt to account for the intricate patterns of stress and vowel alternations in English. In the first presentation of rules for English stress (Chomsky, Halle, and Lukoff, 1956), it was shown that the four or five degrees of stress in English could be accounted for on the basis of a single accent morphophoneme and two kinds of boundary markers. Roughly described, the rules begin with a string of forms in which all the vocalic nuclei are either stressed or unstressed and which are bracketed by numbered boundaries of two kinds: phrase-internal and compound-internal boundaries. A series of rules then reduces the value or weight of the accents either to the right or to the left depending on which kind of boundary is involved. The rules work outward from the smallest parts of the string. At the same time, the order of values is maintained: *bláckbôard* but *blầckbòard jũnglẽ*. Finally, values are assigned to the unaccented vowels, with different values for certain vowels.

When such rules are integrated into a full grammar of English, the function of the special boundary markers is taken over by the representations of constituent structure, i.e., by the P markers. It turns out that significant generalizations can be achieved if the derivational history of the strings can be taken into account. Given such information, and information about the stress patterns produced by various affixes, a series of stress assignment and vowel reduction rules may be applied. These rules account not only for the shape of such items as *telegraph, telegraphy, telegraphic, small boys' school* (with two possible derivations and stress patterns), but also for such apparently disparate facts as the difference in stress and second vowel in such pairs as *torment* and *torrent, condensation* and *compensation*.

Like the rules mentioned above, the rules of stress assignment and reduction operate in a **cycle,** starting from the smallest constituents and carrying out successive erasures of the labeled bracketings (or labeled branches) of the P markers. Thus (to quote an example from Chomsky and Miller, 1963), the rules might operate on a bracketed string such as the following*:

$$
\begin{array}{cccc}
1 & 1 & 1 & 1 \\
\end{array}
$$

[*John's* [[*black board*] *eraser*]   ]
NP   *N N*   *N*   *N NP*

---

*   Here the digits refer not to pitches but to relative stress values, with 1 for primary or heaviest stress, 2 for secondary, and so on.

A rule which assigns dominant stress to the initial position in nouns (i.e., which reduces every other stress by one) applies then to the innermost N and (with subsequent erasure of brackets) yields the next line:

```
      1      1    2    1
   [  John's [ black board eraser ]   ]
   NP       N                  N NP
```

The same rule reapplies to give:

```
      1      1    3    2
   [  John's black board eraser ]
   NP                        NP
```

Eventually, the rules produce the final form:

```
   2      1    4    5 3 5
   John's blackboard eraser
```

The presentation of such cyclical rules has remained largely suggestive and programmatic. Until fuller details have been presented it is impossible to give any final judgment. However, what has appeared has been sufficient to indicate that such processes very likely play an essential role in assigning the proper phonetic shape to the terminal strings of an English grammar. They would go a long way toward explaining the superficially haphazard and complex patterns of English stress. (Full details have been promised in Halle and Chomsky, forthcoming; to supplement the articles mentioned above the reader may consult Chomsky, 1962c.)

We may conclude this brief survey of the various approaches to the phonological component with a mention of the least investigated chapter of phonological theory within a transformational framework: the intonational system of a language like English. Any grammar that purports to enumerate all and only the grammatical sentences of a language must assign possible intonations to its terminal strings. Robert P. Stockwell (1960) has shown that the familiar four-level analysis of English intonation can be integrated into a transformational grammar with considerable ease.

Moreover, even Stockwell's limited and largely programmatic discussion suggests on the one hand that the addition of these phenomena to the described data can play an essential role in decisions as to syntactic analysis. The discussion suggests, on the other hand, that the familiar analysis of English intonation may be modified considerably when it is built into a generative grammar, in the same way that the analysis of English stress may be reinterpreted in a grammar of rules. Finally, we can expect that the interplay of stress and pitch in a language like English (as reflected in the frequent coincidence of primary stress and high pitch in the commonest pitch contours) will eventually be reflected in a set of rules which will account for both kinds of phenomena. (For a comparison and critique of various approaches to phonology from the point of view of transformational theory, see Chomsky, 1962b.)

Problems for Chapter 6

Since most linguistics texts provide detailed discussions of morphological problems, we shall, provide only a few. The reader may find many more examples of limited problems in the workbooks listed before the problems in Chapter 4.

1. Write rules for the following noun forms from the Caucasian language Laz (data from Ralph D. Anderson).

	SINGULAR	PLURAL
sister	dá	dalépe
road	gzá	gzalépe
stone	krá	kralépe
wife	oxórja	oxorjalépe
brother	júma	jumalépe
tongue	néna	nenápe
mother	nána	nanápe
tree	mjá	mjápe
door	nékna	neknápe
hand	xé	xépe
boy	bére	berépe
house	oxóri	oxorépe
apple	uškúri	uškurépe
neck	áli	alépe
man	k'óči	k'očépe
girl	bózo	bozópe

	SINGULAR	PLURAL
chair	órd^{z}u	ord^{z}ópe
face	núk'u	nuk'ópe
who	mí	mípe
what	mú	múpe
head	tí	típe

2. Write morphophonemic rules for English verbs. Assume as input a list of irregular verbs and a few regular ones, and the inflectional formatives Z_3 (third singular), *En* (past participle formant), *Ing*, and *Past*. Use a morphophonemic representation.

3. Write rules for the following partial paradigms of Turkish noun forms.

SINGULAR

NOMINATIVE	gül *rose*	göz *eye*	kilít *lock*	év *house*
POSSESSIVE	gülün	gözün	kilidín	evín
ABLATIVE	güldén	gözdén	kilittén	evdén
DATIVE	gülé	gözé	kilidé	evé

PLURAL

NOMINATIVE	güllér	gözlér	kilitlér	evlér
POSSESSIVE	güllerín	gözlerín	kilitlerín	evlerín
ABLATIVE	güllerdén	gözlerdén	kilitlerdén	evlerdén
DATIVE	gülleré	gözleré	kilitleré	evleré

SINGULAR

NOMINATIVE	bulút *cloud*	kól *arm*	kíz *girl*	yorgán *quilt*
POSSESSIVE	bulutún	kolún	kizín	yorganín
ABLATIVE	buluttán	koldán	kizdán	yorgandán
DATIVE	bulutá	kolá	kizá	yorganá

PLURAL

NOMINATIVE	bulutlár	kollár	kizlár	yorganlár
POSSESSIVE	bulutlarín	kollarín	kizlarín	yorganlarín
ABLATIVE	bulutlardán	kollardán	kizlardár.	yorganlardán
DATIVE	bulutlará	kollará	kizlará	yorganlará

SINGULAR

NOMINATIVE	kedí *cat*	halí *rug*	akíl *intelligence*	aklí *his intelligence*
POSSESSIVE	kedinín	halinín	aklín	aklinín
ABLATIVE	kedidén	halidán	akildán	aklindán
DATIVE	kediyé	haliyá	aklá	akliná

PLURAL

NOMINATIVE	kedilér	halilár	akillár	akillarí
POSSESSIVE	kedilerín	halilarín	akillarín	akillarinín
ABLATIVE	kedilerdén	halilardán	akillardán	akillarindán
DATIVE	kedileré	halilará	akillará	akilariná

SINGULAR

NOMINATIVE	eví *his house*	halisí *his rug*	gülű *his rose*
POSSESSIVE	evinín	halisinín	gözünűn *his eye*
ABLATIVE	evindén	halisindán	kedisindén *his cat*
DATIVE	eviné	halisiná	bulutuná *his cloud*

PLURAL

NOMINATIVE	evlerí	halilarí	kollarí *his arms*
POSSESSIVE	evlerinín	halilarinín	kizlarinín *his girls*
ABLATIVE	evlerindén	halilarindán	yorganlarindán *his quilts*
DATIVE	evleriné	halilariná	kilitleriné *his locks*

SINGULAR

NOMINATIVE	lokánta *restaurant*	gülűm *my rose*
POSSESSIVE	lokántanin	gözümün *my eye*
ABLATIVE	lokántadan	kedimdén *my cat*
DATIVE	lokántaya	bulutumá *my cloud*

PLURAL

NOMINATIVE	lokántalarim *my restaurants*	kollarim *my arms*
POSSESSIVE	lokántalarimin	kizlarimin *my girls*
ABLATIVE	lokántalarimdan	yorganlarimdán *my quilts*
DATIVE	lokántalarima	kilitlerimé *my locks*

4. Write rules for the following Japanese forms (numerals and classifiers).*
Forms are given in a (fairly broad) phonetic transcription. ($\underset{\circ}{V}$ = voiceless
vowel; $\tilde{V}$ = nasalized vowel.)

Numerals	Set I	Set II	vehicles	cupfuls
one	ičį	çįtot$^\text{s}$į	ičidai	ippai
two	ni	φųtat$^\text{s}$į	nidai	nihai
three	saã	mitt$^\text{s}$į	sanndai	sammbai
four	ši	yott$^\text{s}$į	yonndai	yoõhai
five	go	it$^\text{s}$įt$^\text{s}$į	godai	gohai
six	roku	mutt$^\text{s}$į	rokudai	roppai
seven	šįči	nanat$^\text{s}$į	nanadai/šįčidai†	šįčihai
eight	hačį	yatt$^\text{s}$į	hačidai	happai
nine	kyuu	kokonot$^\text{s}$į	kyuudai	kyuuhai
ten	juu	too	juudai	jippai
how many	ikut$^\text{s}$į	nanndai	nammbai

---

* Based on Samuel E. Martin, *Essential Japanese*, rev. ed. (Rutland, Vt.,
Charles E. Tuttle Co., Inc., 1956).

† And in general for every form in *šiči*, there exists an alternate form with
nana, and vice versa.

hundreds	cows, horses, and so on	volumes	pages
ippyakų	ittoo	issatˢį	ippeiji
nihyakų	nitoo	nisatˢį	nipeiji
sammbyakų	sanntoo	saāsatˢį	sammpeiji
yoōhyakų	yonntoo	yoōsatˢį	yommpeiji
gohyakų	gotoo	gosatˢį	gopeiji
roppyakų	rokųtoo	rokųsatˢį	rokųpeiji
nanahyakų	nanatoo	nanasatˢį	nanapeiji
happyakų	hattoo	hačįsatˢį	happeiji
kyuuhyakų	kyuutoo	kyuusatˢį	kyuupeiji
—	jittoo	jissatˢį	jippeiji
nammbyakų	nanntoo	naāsatˢį	nammpeiji

birds	persons	boxfuls	days
ičiwa	çįtori	çįtohako	ičiniči
niwa	φųtari	φųtahako	φųtˢįka
sammba	sannnii	mihako	mikka
yowa/yoōwa/ yommba	yonii/yottari	yohako	yokka
gowa	gonii	itˢįhako	itˢįka
roppa/rokuwa	rokunii	muhako	muika
nanawa	nananii	nanahako	nanoka/nanuka
happa/hačiwa	hačinii	yahako	yooka
kyuuwa	kyuunii	kokonohako	kokonoka
jippa	juunii	tohako/toohako	tooka
nammba	nannnii	ikųhako	nannniči

CHAPTER SEVEN

THE FORM OF GRAMMARS

7.1 Mathematics and Linguistics

Perhaps the most lasting result of the linguistic research of the last decade will be the acquisition of the language and techniques of modern logic and mathematics for the discussion of fundamental linguistic problems. The impetus for this development came partly from outside linguistics: from logicians concerned with various abstract "language systems," to a lesser extent from telephone engineers interested in studying the mathematical properties of various codes and transmission systems, and from computer technologists trying to solve the problem of machine translation and other related problems of high-speed data processing. But much more important has been the internal development of linguistics. Such widely differing schools of linguists as the Prague circle, glossematicians, and American structuralists have all concurred in insisting that languages be studied as structures, that is, as networks of relationships. Similarly, a great part of the linguistic literature of the last thirty or forty years has been concerned with discussing the character of the fundamental notions of linguistic analysis, very often in the form of attempts to state a set of criteria, or a set of postulates (axioms) from which particular applications of linguistic theory would follow.

To document this bit of cultural history in detail would take us well beyond the bounds of this introduction. The foregoing remarks are meant to refer not just to generative and transformational linguistics, but to something that can be referred to only by the vague phrase "the development of linguistic thought in general." Such a development does not take place in a straight line, and the numerous blind alleys and negative results play a part as do the positive achievements. Thus, the information-theoretic model of communication proposed by Shannon (see Shannon and Weaver, 1949) caused a brief flurry of excitement among linguists, but was soon shown to be a special case of an elementary type of grammar, a finite-state system (see Section 7.4) that is demonstrably inadequate for the description of a natural language. This negative result was of some importance, since the same model (in the form of morpheme and morpheme-sequence charts) was currently widely used and proposed for syntactic descriptions. A positive effect then was the search for more adequate models for syntactic theories formulated in as precise a way as the finite-state model. Similarly, although machine translation has as yet scarcely contributed any basic insights into linguistic structure, it has had the result of convincing many linguists of the inadequacy and inexplicitness of much of current linguistic theory and current descriptions of particular languages. Further, it has had the not unimportant practical effect of providing a meeting ground for mathematicians and linguists.

For the discipline which is most concerned with structures in general is mathematics. And a large part of the mathematical-logical energies of the last century has been directed at the abstract study of various axiom systems and their relations. Modern symbolic logic and mathematics (which are really two ends of the same study) offer to the linguist a wide array of ideas and methods which he can ill afford to ignore. Up until rather recently most logicians who concerned themselves at all with natural languages showed themselves to be totally ignorant of modern linguistics. Their conception of grammar as it was conceived in the eighteenth century was matched by the linguists' idea of logic as something completely unrelated to linguistic description, an idea in turn based primarily on pre-Fregean logic. There have been, of course, notable exceptions. Now all this has changed. The reader of the standard linguistic journals is apt to find articles in any issue that demand considerable mathematical sophistication on his part. Conversely, many of the fundamental papers referred to in the linguistic literature of recent years will be found in technical journals for radio engineers, communication theorists, and logicians. At several universities and institutes courses in "mathematical linguistics" are offered. Of course, a wide variety of subject matters can be covered by this term (for a recent survey, see Plath, 1961).

Unfortunately, the training of most linguists has not included any work either in modern logic or mathematics. And the parts of logic and mathematics that are most relevant to the theory of grammars are usually not treated in elementary courses. The inevitable result of this situation has been a lack of communication, evident at many public gatherings of linguists. It is to be hoped that this situation will be ameliorated by more training in mathematics for linguists and by more serious attempts to explain the new ideas and methods to the mathematical layman. Much could be done by the creation of specialized courses for linguistics students covering those parts of mathematics that are relevant. But it is impossible to predict just what parts of the whole gamut of mathematical-logical studies may turn out to be crucial for advances of linguistics in the future.

It should be emphasized that the considerations of this chapter relate primarily to discussions of general linguistic theory and to the abstract study of grammatical systems. For the construction of transformational grammars for particular languages nothing whatsoever in the way of a mathematical background is necessary. A certain amount of facility in handling symbols and practice in manipulating the notational conventions is all that is needed, and the same statement would hold for any kind of linguistic work.

I cannot hope to give anything like a complete introduction to the mathematics of languages and grammars in this brief chapter. Rather, I shall merely outline a few fundamental considerations and guide the reader to various works which he can profitably use to help him through the more abstruse literature that has appeared.

First of all, it must be understood that pure mathematics and logic are not concerned with statements of the form "such and such is true, therefore something else is true," but rather with statements of the form "if such and such is true, then something else is also true." That is, a mathematical discipline is concerned with studying the consequences that follow from the *assumption* of various sets of primitive terms and statements. (It is immaterial whether the primitive statements are considered to be true *a priori*, or simply accepted as rules of the game from which one starts.) In a completely formalized system the relation of being a "consequence" is stated explicitly, i.e., there are explicit rules for defining terms on the basis of the primitive terms and explicit rules for deriving statements (theorems) from the basic unproved axioms of the theory. Except where the system is itself concerned with the most basic parts of mathematical theory (i.e., logic), the fundamental apparatus of logic is assumed as available. But in principle, any mathematical discipline can be formalized in this way simply by adding the appropriate parts of logical theory to its list of axioms and primitive terms.

Parenthetically, we may note the close analogy between such a mathematical system and the structure of a grammar as it has been presented here. Parallel to the logical system underlying any mathematical theory is the general theory of grammars which tells us the meaning of our various symbols ($\rightarrow$, { }, and so forth), and how to manipulate the rules to derive sentences. The sentences are parallel to the theorems of the mathematical system. The empirical linguistic problem is to find the most appropriate terms and rules which can account for the "theorems" given by the native speaker (or extracted from what is given).

The use of special symbols and mathematical notations is not essential, although practically it is of great importance. That is, the use of mathematical symbols does not make a theory mathematical any more than stating a chemical theory in Spanish would make the theory "Spanish" (except in a rather unimportant sense). Conversely, any mathematical theory could be stated in ordinary language, although this would often make it incomprehensible. Moreover, ordinary language is often so vague that using a familiar term with a special meaning makes for more difficulties than does the use of a special sign. Much of the difficulty encountered in the literature of recent linguistic theory arises simply from the use of symbols and terms with precise but special meanings familiar to mathematicians but not to most linguistics. Furthermore, mathematical writing is usually done in a very closely packed style with much left to the reader in the way of supplying proofs, pondering supposedly "obvious" statements, and making the transition to results that "follow immediately" from foregoing arguments. Here, the linguist who has exercised his patience by reading some of the denser chapters of modern linguistic theory or working through modern structural sketches is in a somewhat better state of preparation. (Some general introductions to logic and the structure of mathematical systems are Quine, 1951; Carnap, 1958; Rosenbloom, 1950. Of these Carnap is the most complete; Rosenbloom assumes the most in mathematical background. None provide any help in discovering the particular applications to linguistic theory.)

To illustrate how some of the concepts of logic and mathematics can enter into linguistic discussion, we may informally consider several examples drawn from elementary but basic parts of modern logic.

★7.2   Set Theory

Much of the discussion of linguistic theory of the last decades has used the terminology of classes. Phonemes have been considered by some to be classes of sounds, morphemes as classes of morphs, and so on. The abstract study of the notions involved in such a

view is called **set theory.** The fundamental notion in this theory
is the relation of **set** (class) **membership,** symbolized by $\in$ (for
Greek ἐστί 'is'). Thus, we may write $x \in M$ to mean "x is a
member of the set M." If we wish to say that x is not a member of
the set M, we write $x \notin M$. Braces are often used to denote a set;
e.g., $\{x, y, z\}$ denotes the set consisting of x, y, and z. Order of
listing is immaterial: $\{x, z, y\}$ is the same set as the one just
given.

Two sets are considered **equal** $(M = N)$ if and only if they
contain the same elements. We say that a set M is **included** in
(is a **subset** of) another set N if every member of M is also a
member of N; i.e., for every x, if $x \in M$, then $x \in N$. In symbols
this is expressed as $M \subseteq N$. Further, if M is a subset of N and is
not equal to N, we say that M is **properly included** in (is a **proper
part** or **proper subset** of) N. In symbols this is expressed as $M \subset N$.
The relation of inclusion is to be sharply distinguished from the
relation of set membership, otherwise much confusion results. Sets
can themselves be members of sets, of course. These distinctions
are not usually reflected in ordinary language. We use the same
linguistic form for membership and for inclusion: "This armadillo
is a mammal" ($\in$); "The armadillo is a mammal" (i.e., "armadillos
are mammals": $\subseteq$).

(The reader will probably encounter several other logical signs
in formulations such as we have made in the last paragraph. These
come from general logical theory: $\equiv$ to mean "if and only if,"
(x) to mean "for any x"; and $(\exists_x)$ to mean "there is at least one
x." Thus we might write

$$\{(M, N)[M \subset N]\}$$
$$\equiv \{(M \subseteq N) \quad \text{and} \quad (\exists_x)(x \in N \quad \text{and} \quad x \notin M)\}$$

to mean "for any two sets M and N, M is a proper part of N if and
only if M is included in N and there is an x such that x is a member
of N and x is not a member of M." Other signs frequently used:
· for "and"; ∨ for logical disjunction, i.e., "or" in the nonexclusive
sense; → or ⊃ for "if · · · then." We shall not use these signs below.)

Two sets are of special importance, the **null** or empty set
(ø or Λ), which is included in every set, and the **universal** set (for
some universe of discourse, denoted often by U), which has the
property that every set is included in it. The set of x's such that
$x \not\in M$ is called the **complement** of M, in symbols M' or $\sim M$.

Two (or more) sets can be used to form a new set by the following operations. The **intersection** or **logical product** of two sets
M and N is the set of those objects that are members of both
M and N; in symbols $M \cap N$. If $M \cap N = ø$, then M and N are
said to be **disjoint**, i.e., they have no members in common. It is
always the case that $M \cap M' = ø$. The **union** or **logical sum** of
two sets is the set of objects that belong to either one (or both),
in symbols $M \cup N$. The union of a set and its complement is the
universal set, i.e., $M \cup M' = U$. There is an obvious relationship
between these two operations and two of the logical relations
holding between statements. The intersection of two sets is the
set of objects of which it is true to state that they belong to one
set *and* the other set. The union is the set of which it can be said
that its members belong to one set *or* the other (in the nonexclusive
sense usual in logic). ("Or" in the exclusive sense has its counterpart in $+$: $M + N = (M \cup N) \cap (M \cap N)'$ is the set of those
objects that are members of either M or N but not both.)

To illustrate, if L stands for the set of all linguists and M the
set of all mathematicians, then $L \cup M$ is the set of all people who
are either linguists or mathematicians. If $L \cap M$ is not empty —
if there is at least one person who is both a mathematician and a
linguist — then L and M are not disjoint. If it were the case that
every mathematician were also a linguist then it would be true
that $M \subseteq L$ and $M \cap L = M$.

A third operation is the formation of a new set — the **Cartesian
product** — of all ordered pairs (or triples, and so on) (x, y) from
two (or three, or more) sets M and N such that $x \in M$ and $y \in N$,
in symbols $M \times N$. Notice the difference in meaning between the
parentheses and braces, the former being used to enclose an
ordered set (pair, triple, and so on, an ordered sequence of n items

being called an *n*-tuple). When a rule of grammar has the form

$$X \rightarrow \begin{Bmatrix} x \\ x' \end{Bmatrix} \begin{Bmatrix} y \\ y' \\ y'' \end{Bmatrix}$$

the rule allows us to form the Cartesian product of the two sets; e.g., (x, y), (x, y'), (x, y''), (x', y), and so forth.

Sets consisting of a single member are perfectly respectable, although we must distinguish sharply between the element x and the set $\{x\}$. Every set is included in itself. On the other hand, no set can contain itself as a member, or else various paradoxes will result: the set of all linguists is not itself a linguist.

Sets may be defined in either of two ways, by listing all their members (extensionally) or by naming some property shared by every member of the class and no others (intensionally). In the latter instance, the usual notation is $\{x \mid Px\}$ where Px stands for a statement giving the defining property and $\mid$ may be read "such that." For instance, we might denote the class of residents of Texas (with x understood to have values chosen from the set of human beings, or, as is sometimes said, to "range over" human beings) by $\{x \mid x$ lives in Texas$\}$. Either of these methods is permissible, but they will obviously not always be equally appropriate or feasible. If a set is infinite we cannot list it exhaustively, although we can in some instances provide an explicit procedure for listing its members up to any desired number. For instance, the set of all positive integers $(1, 2, 3, \cdots)$ is (denumerably) infinite. If we denote 1 by 1, 2 by $1'$, 3 by $1''$, and so on, we can provide a rule enumerating the integers (i.e., the N's):

$$N \rightarrow \begin{Bmatrix} N' \\ 1 \end{Bmatrix}$$

In the view presented in this book, a grammar is an attempt to construct explicit rules of this sort for the often nonfinite classes of linguistic forms in a given language. All the classes are defined extensionally, or by means of such recursive processes.

One of the results of set theory has been the differentiation of various kinds of infinite sets. The "smallest" kind of infinite set is a set which is denumerable or countable, that is, which can be put into one-to-one correspondence with the set of all positive integers. Such sets have the somewhat surprising property that they have the same number of elements as various sets which are properly included in them, e.g., the set of all positive integers and the set of all even numbers. The set of all sequences of any length constructed out of a finite set of elements is denumerable. Since we have defined a language to be a subset of such a set, we know that the set of all sentences in a language is (at most) denumerable. On the other hand, the set of all possible languages constructed out of a finite set of elements (with no length limit) is not denumerable. This follows from a theorem of set theory which states that the set of all subsets of a set always has a higher number (or "power") than the set itself. Further, if all grammars are finite in length, then the set of all grammars is denumerable. It follows that there must be languages (in the abstract sense) which have no grammars (Chomsky and Miller, 1958).

A great deal of energy has been spent in the last few decades on trying to find intensional definitions for classes of linguistic items, that is, to provide descriptions of the form "the class of x's such that Px." Naturally, such a description is useful to the extent that the property denoted by P is well defined. For this reason definitions in terms of meaning are ruled out. If *Noun* is the class of x's such that x means a person, place, or thing, then we are faced with the difficult task of deciding whether a given x (e.g., *function*) does or does not mean a person, place, or thing. It is important to notice that even in such an approach, when we encounter a word like *function*, which does not fit the defining properties, we do not conclude that it is not a noun, but rather we reject the definition and search for a more adequate one. That is, we know ahead of time in some sense what we want to come out with as the result of our analysis. This is one sense in which it can be said that linguistic analysis tries to account for the linguistic intuition of the native speaker.

Having found meaning to be inadequate, linguists attempted to find formal properties and relations to define their classes. Thus, one might begin to describe the class of adjectives as $\{x \mid x, x\text{-}er,$ and $x\text{-}est$ are words in English$\}$. Assuming for the sake of the argument that "word in English" is well defined, this description is seen to be inadequate by such cases as *on, honor, honest, note, noter, noticed* or by the exclusion of *good, bad,* and so forth. At this point (expanding the definition rather than accepting its consequences), some investigators reintroduce meaning: *Adjective* is the set of x's and y's such that $x, x\text{-}er, x\text{-}est$ and $y, y\text{-}er, y\text{-}est$ are words in English and the meaning of x is to the meaning of $x\text{-}er$ is to the meaning of $x\text{-}est$ as the meaning of y is to the meaning of $y\text{-}er$ is to the meaning of $y\text{-}est$. But it is difficult to see in what sense *long, longer, longest* have differences of meaning that are proportional to the differences of *short, shorter, shortest,* except in a sense which will lead to circularity (i.e., we define the meanings of positive, comparative, superlative on the basis of *Adjective,* and *Adjective* on the basis of these meanings). Hence, others attempt to avoid these difficulties by recourse to the notion of distribution. Since this term is used so often in describing various criteria for classifications, it is worthwhile analyzing it to see whether it really solves the problem.

The distribution of a given form is the class of environments in which the form occurs. Environment means whatever is left when we extract the form from a sequence; e.g., the environment of *hot* in *It's hot in here* is *It's* ———— *in here.* We must settle first of all the meaning of "the class of environments in which the form occurs." Does this mean a given corpus or the set of all possible environments? In the first instance, the distribution of a given form will be a finite set; in the second, presumably a denumerably infinite set. Let us consider first the case of a finite distribution. We must assume first that the corpus is segmented into short sequences. This is a big assumption and one may ask: How short? For if it is not, then the distribution of each form will merely be n listings of the corpus minus the form (where n is the number of occurrences of the form). No two forms will have the same distribution. The corpus, then, is broken up into shorter sequences. Now, any given corpus will be incomplete in a more or less accidental manner, unless it has been carefully prepared to contain all the possible combinations (up to some longest sequence). In practice, of course, the linguist attempts to round out the corpus by making substitutions, that is, by extending the distributions of various items. But if carried out to the full extent, this means that the linguist is attempting to project an infinite distribution for most of his forms. The case of a truly bounded distribution occurs in historical work but does not in principle differ from the description of a living language. The historical linguist merely has to rely more on guesses and indirect evidence as to whether his projections are valid (and is, in fact, predicting that no newly discovered documents will prove him wrong).

We are led then to the other alternative in any case. Intensional definitions will reduce to the form $\{x \mid Dx\}$ where D stands for the distribution of the class. But since D is infinite for most linguistic classes, we are faced with precisely the problem of a generative grammar; namely, to give a series of rules, necessarily recursive, which will enumerate the members of D for a given class. The rules will specify the possible and denumerably infinite distributions for each of the forms of the language. The great difference between this view and some other views of linguistics is that in the generative approach this specification by rules is seen as the primary task of linguistic description. In the other views, the statement of various *ad hoc* criteria by which the forms of a language can be classified is seen as the primary task of linguistic description. (In the generative approach classification will follow ideally from such general criteria as simplicity.)

Actually, most distributional "definitions" (including the use of the so-called diagnostic frames technique) do not form parts of a grammar in our sense at all. They are rather directions as to how, working with a native speaker, one might go about assembling data for a grammar. If we attempt to put such definitions into our theories, we are reduced to the absurdity of such grammars as the following (meant literally as a grammar): "Whatever John Smith says is an English sentence."

These remarks should not be taken to imply that the techniques of substitution and the comparison of distributions for various linguistic forms are irrelevant to the task of constructing a grammar. They are relevant to the extent that any kind of data-processing techniques are relevant to scientific work. Linguists who study syntax will have to process huge amounts of material. In such study — as the various machine translation projects have shown — the problems of data searching and comparison can become crucial. Various techniques of the sort that have come to be called computational linguistics (from the use of electronic computers) will undoubtedly play an ever greater role in linguistic research. (The reader will find some discussion of the algebra of classes in the general introductions to symbolic logic mentioned above. Two more detailed introductions to set theory are Kamke, 1962; and Suppes, 1960. On definitions and related matters see Hempel, 1952.)

★7.3   The Theory of Relations

Set theory alone is inadequate as a mathematical tool for studying linguistic structure. A language cannot be considered to be merely a hierarchy of classes of items, classes of classes, and so on. Let us consider briefly another chapter from modern logical theory, namely, the theory of relations.

Like the notion of a class, the notion of a relation is so fundamental that we can scarcely define it in terms of some underlying, more basic idea (although it can be defined in terms of ordered sets). Relations hold between two or more terms and are accordingly named dyadic, triadic (or, for *n* terms, *n*-adic) or binary, ternary, and so on. "Giving" is a triadic relation. "John knows more about linguistics than Mike knows about basket weaving" illustrates a relation with four terms. But most discussion of relations is confined to two-placed relations: "equals," "is greater than," "is the father of," "precedes." Like classes, relations can be considered intensionally or extensionally. In the latter case, a relation is the set of ordered pairs (triples, n-tuples) for which it holds. An essential property of a relation is that it has a direction or sense; the sets of terms of which it holds are ordered sets.

We may denote a relation by a capital letter (or capitalized word) and the terms of which it holds by lower-case letters in parentheses. Thus $R(a, b)$ stands for "a has the relation R to b." The class of all first-place terms for a given relation is called the **domain** of the relation. The class of all second-place terms for a (dyadic) relation is called the **converse domain** or **range** of the relation. The union of the domain and the range is called the **field** of the relation. For instance, if F stands for the relation of being the (human) father of someone, then the domain of F is the class of all fathers; the range (and field) of F is the class of all humans.

A relation is said to be **reflexive** if for every x in its domain it is the case that $R(x, x)$, i.e., if it holds for an individual it always holds between that individual and itself. If no term has the relation to itself, then it is called **irreflexive**. If there is at least one term in its domain that does not bear the relation to itself, then it is classed as **nonreflexive**. *Smaller-or-equal* is reflexive. *Smaller* is irreflexive, and *Admiring* is presumably nonreflexive; i.e., there are some people who admire someone and do not admire themselves.

A relation R is said to be **symmetric** if for every x and y, $R(x, y)$ implies $R(y, x)$; a relation is **asymmetric** if it never is the case that both $R(x, y)$ and $R(y, x)$; it is **nonsymmetric** if there is at least one pair such that $R(x, y)$ and not $R(y, x)$. *Smaller-or-equal* is symmetric, as is *Equal; Smaller* is asymmetric; and *Loving* is nonsymmetric, as numerous poems testify.

A relation R is said to be **transitive** if for every x, y, z, $R(x, y)$ and $R(y, z)$ imply $R(x, z)$. **Intransitive** and **nontransitive** are defined in a way parallel to the other terms above. *Equal, Smaller* are transitive; *Father* is an intransitive relation; *Friend* is nontransitive if you are my friend and have friends who are not my friends.

Finally, we say that a relation R is **connex** (or **connected**) if for any two distinct members of its field either $R(x, y)$ or $R(y, x)$. Thus, for numbers the relation *Smaller* is connex.

Another set of distinctions leads to the definition of various kinds of ordering relations. A **series** (or serial relation) is a relation which is transitive, irreflexive, and connex (or equivalently, transitive, asymmetric, and connex), as for example the relation *Precedes* holding between elements in a string. Of every two items a, b in a string, either a precedes b or b precedes a (connectivity). No item precedes itself (irreflexivity). If a precedes b, then b does not precede a (asymmetry). If a precedes b and b precedes c, then a precedes c (transitivity). It is clear that we are talking here of occurrences of items. The important distinction between an item and an occurrence of an item is often denoted by the distinction between a **type** (or sign design) — the phoneme /a/ — and a **token** (or sign occurrence) — the occurrence of /a/ in the second position of a particular utterance of the word /pat/.

Another type of ordering is designated by the term **partial order.** A relation, R, is called a partial order if it is reflexive and transitive and if for any two distinct members x and y it cannot be the case that both $R(x, y)$ and $R(y, x)$. (Where $R(x, y)$ and $R(y, x)$ always imply identity of x and y the relation is called **antisymmetric.**) The relation *Dominates* defined on nodes (as tokens) of a P marker (Section 4.4) is a partial order. A relation which is a partial order and is connex in addition is called a **simple order.** The relation *Less-than-or-equal* ($\leq$) for the natural numbers is a simple ordering.

Relations which are transitive, symmetric, and (hence) reflexive make up an important type called **equivalence relations.** Familiar examples are *Equals*, *Similar*, and so on. The relation of phonemic conformity is likewise an equivalence relation (the relation that holds between two utterances that are phonemically "same").

It is evident that the theory of relations provides a much richer language for linguistic discussion than does the theory of sets alone. What are called constructions in languages may be considered complex classes of relations. For instance, *Prepositional phrase* in

English is usually a two-termed relation $P(x, y)$ with its domain the set of all prepositions in English, and its range (or converse domain) the set of all noun phrases (and some adverbs). *Noun phrase* in turn is a complex class consisting of (1) the class of proper names, (2) the relation *Objective pronoun* holding between the set of pronouns and the set of objective case affixes for pronouns (assuming that they are thus analyzed), (3) all other types of noun phrases, which form in turn a complex (and nonfinite) class of classes, relations such as *Definite nominal, Adjectivally modified nominal,* and so on. In Chapter 5 we considered various types of relations in languages.

⋆7.4 The Hierarchy of Grammars

So far in this chapter we have been concerned only with showing that the mathematical disciplines offer a precise language for discussing many of the fundamental ideas of linguistic theory. (An example of the use of set theory and relation theory for the discussion of phonemics is found in Peterson and Harary, 1961.) Some other branches of mathematics that have entered into recent linguistic discussions are those of graph theory (Berge, 1958) and recursive function theory (Davis, 1958; Goodstein, 1957). Also, many terms and ideas from modern algebra have been used (Birkhoff and MacLane, 1953). I am ignoring here many areas not directly related to the theory of grammars, such as information theory and lexicostatistics.

In the remainder of the chapter we shall take one further step and show something of the nature and techniques of the mathematical study of grammars. As in any pure mathematical study, we can proceed by setting up certain basic terms and axioms and studying the consequences of these axioms. As an example we may take an article by Noam Chomsky, "On Certain Formal Properties of Grammars" (1959a). I shall quote a portion of this article giving part of the initial set of terms and axioms, explain the notions involved, and then outline the main argument of the article.

The basic system of description that we shall consider is a system G of the following form: G is a semi-group under concatenation [see below] with strings in a finite set V of symbols as its elements, and I as the identity element. V is called the "vocabulary" of G. $V = V_T \cup V_N$ (V_T, V_N disjoint), where V_T is the "terminal vocabulary" and V_N the "nonterminal vocabulary." V_T contains I and a "boundary" element $\#$. V_N contains an element S (sentence). A two-place relation $\rightarrow$ is defined on elements of G, read "can be rewritten as." This relation satisfies the following conditions:

AXIOM 1. $\rightarrow$ is irreflexive.

AXIOM 2. $A \in V_N$ if and only if there are φ, ψ, ω such that $\varphi A \psi \rightarrow \varphi \omega \psi$.

AXIOM 3. There are no φ, ψ, ω such that $\varphi \rightarrow \psi \# \omega$.

AXIOM 4. There is a finite set of pairs $(\chi_1, \omega_1), \cdots, (\chi_n, \omega_n)$ such that for all φ, ψ, $\varphi \rightarrow \psi$ if and only if there are φ_1, φ_2, and $j \leq n$ [i.e. less than or equal to n] such that $\varphi = \varphi_1 \chi_j \varphi_2$ and $\psi = \varphi_1 \omega_j \varphi_2$.

Thus the pairs (χ_j, ω_j) whose existence is guaranteed by Axiom 4 give a finite specification of the relation $\rightarrow$. In other words, we may think of the grammar as containing a finite number of rules $\chi_j \rightarrow \omega_j$ which completely determine all possible derivations.*

It is evident that a good deal of special knowledge on the reader's part is assumed here as well as considerable facility in absorbing condensed formulation. Most of the special symbols and terms have been explained here already ("disjoint," $\in$, $\cup$). It will be recalled from Chapter 2 that the identity (or null) element I is the element with the property that for any string x, $x + I = I + x = x$. The statement that G is a semi-group is simply equivalent to a further set of axioms regarding the operation of concatenation. A group in modern algebra is a system with an equivalence relation and a binary operation such that for any two elements in the system a new element can be formed from them which is also in the system. In a group the operation must be associative, that is, for all elements x, y, z (taking & as symbol for the operation), $x \mathbin{\&} (y \mathbin{\&} z) = (x \mathbin{\&} y) \mathbin{\&} z$. There must be an identity element, and there must be for every element x an inverse x' such that $x \mathbin{\&} x' = I$.

---

* *Information and Control* 2.137–67 (1959). I am indebted to the Academic Press, Inc., and Professor Chomsky for permission to quote this passage from p. 141.

In ordinary multiplication the identity element is 1 and the inverse of every number x (except 0) is the reciprocal $1/x$. In a **semi-group** for a given binary operation (if the operation is concatenation as here, it is also called a script or concatenation algebra) there need not be an inverse (see Rosenbloom, 1950, p. 189; or Davis, 1958, p. 95). Ordinary arithmetical multiplication and addition form groups of a special character called commutative (or Abelian) groups, since they obey the commutative law: $x + y = y + x$; semi-groups are in general noncommutative.

The paper continues by defining a number of further terms, of which we need mention only two: the relation *dominates* ($\Rightarrow$), with which we are already familiar (Section 4.4); the relation of (weak) **equivalence** holding between two grammars (i.e., systems of the form G) just in case they generate the same language. Two grammars are said to be **strongly equivalent** if they generate not only the same set of strings but the same set of structural descriptions — e.g., P markers — for the strings (Chomsky and Miller, 1963). It is the simpler notion of weak equivalence that has played a greater part in the mathematical study of grammars, whereas the notion of strong equivalence has entered largely into discussions of the empirical adequacy of grammatical systems — e.g., the discussion of recursive adjective rules in PS grammars (see Section 4.3). The latter notion is ultimately of far greater interest for linguistics. (It should be noted that the use of the symbol $\Rightarrow$ to denote the relation of domination has nothing to do with the use of a double arrow in transformational rules mentioned above, Section 4.2.)

The main body of the paper is concerned with adding additional restrictions to the axioms given above and with studying the relations between the grammars and languages obeying these further restrictions. We may paraphrase these additional restrictions as follows:

RESTRICTION 1. Every rule (i.e., every pair of Axiom 4) is of the form $xAy \rightarrow xwy$ where A is a single symbol, w is not I, and x and y may be equal to I.

RESTRICTION 2. Every rule is of the form $xAy \rightarrow xwy$, with A and w as in Restriction 1, but x and y must be null.

RESTRICTION 3. Every rule is of the form $xAy \rightarrow xwy$ with A, x, y as in Restriction 2, but w is not null and is either a single terminal symbol, a, or a single terminal symbol plus a single nonterminal symbol, i.e. aB.

A grammar with none of these three restrictions is called a Type 0 grammar, and grammars obeying each of the three restrictions respectively are called Type 1, Type 2, and Type 3 grammars. A language with a Type 0 grammar is called a Type 0 language, and so on. Following somewhat later usage (Chomsky, 1963), we may call the Type 0 grammars "unrestricted rewriting systems" (UR). It will be apparent that the Type 1 grammars are context-sensitive (CS) phrase-structure grammars; Type 2 grammars are context-free (CF) PS grammars. A Type 3 grammar (as is shown in the article) is what has been called elsewhere a finite-state (FS) grammar (Chomsky, 1956, 1957; Chomsky and Miller, 1958).

The first theorem, which follows from the definitions, states that for both grammars and languages Type FS $\subseteq$ Type CF $\subseteq$ Type CS $\subseteq$ Type UR. That is, the relation of class inclusion holds in the order given among these four types of systems. The succeeding argument is aimed at showing that the relation between these classes of grammars and languages is proper inclusion, i.e., that Type FS $\subset$ Type CF $\subset$ Type CS $\subset$ Type UR. For grammars, this result follows simply from inspecting the definitions of the types of rules in each kind of grammar (i.e., the result follows "trivially"). To show that the relation holds also for the generated languages, it is necessary to prove that there are languages which can be generated by UR grammars which cannot be generated by CS grammars, and so on for CS and CF, CF and FS grammars.

The initial comparison between unrestricted rewriting systems and context-sensitive grammars draws upon results of a branch of mathematics known as recursive function theory — a discipline which studies, for instance, whether a certain function is computable or whether a mechanical procedure for solving a certain problem is possible. In general, the discipline is concerned with the theory of abstract automata such as Turing machines (not actual computing machines, but mathematical systems that can be conceptualized as machines). A Turing machine is a system that can be thought of as a machine with a finite number of internal states, a paper tape divided into a number of squares, a device for splicing on extra tape at either end whenever it is needed, a scanner which can scan one square at a time, and a set of symbols that can be printed onto or read off the squares. The system consists of a set of instructions of the following form (these remarks apply to what are called simple Turing machines):

$$State_i \qquad Symbol_j \qquad X \qquad State_l$$

where X is either a symbol or R or L, and the instruction means "given the internal state $State_i$ and the scanned $Symbol_j$, change the internal state to $State_l$ (which may be the same as $State_i$). Then do one of three things: if X is a symbol, replace $Symbol_j$ by this symbol; if X is R, scan the next square to the right; if X is L, scan the next square to the left." One condition on Turing machines is that no two instructions have the same first two members; that is, given an internal state and a scanned symbol, the next move is unambiguously determined. (For a clear explanation designed for the nonmathematician see Davis, 1958; see also Chomsky, 1963, with special reference to the theory of grammars.)

Returning to our article, Chomsky next states (without proof, but referring to a relevant section of Davis, 1958) that "every recursively enumerable set of strings is a Type 0 [UR] language (and conversely)." He shows further that every CS language is a decidable (or recursive) set of strings. A **recursively enumerable** set is a set which can be generated by a Turing machine. A **decidable** set of strings is a set such that after a finite number of steps it is possible to determine whether or not a given string is in the set. Because Restriction 1 guarantees that of two succeeding lines in a derivation the second will always be at least as long as the first, we can always tell for any string of finite length whether or not it is derivable from the grammar simply by examining all (finitely many) possible derivations of strings no longer than the string in question. One of the results of recursive function theory is that there are recursively enumerable sets which are not decidable (whereas every decidable set is recursively enumerable). Therefore the set of CS languages is properly included in the set of UR languages.

The proof of the next theorem is preceded by two preliminary steps (lemmas). In the first lemma it is shown that for every grammar formed from a CS grammar by adding a permutational rule $(xy \rightarrow yx)$ there exists an equivalent CS grammar. In other words, without violating Restriction 1 it is possible to have a series of rules having the effect only of rearranging two adjacent strings (see Section 3.3). In the second lemma, a language of essentially the form $\# a^n b^m a^n b^m \#$ (where a^n means a string of n a's) is shown by actual construction of a grammar to be a CS language. We may derive this language by the following grammar (somewhat simpler than Chomsky's):

Given: $\# S \#$

1. $S \rightarrow A(S_1)aB(S_2)b$
2. $S_1 \rightarrow A(S_1)a$
3. $S_2 \rightarrow B(S_2)b$
4. $aB \rightarrow Ba$
5. $A \rightarrow a$
6. $B \rightarrow b$

(Chomsky's construction is a grammar for a language of the form $\# a^n b^m a^n b^m ccc \#$ where ccc is the reflex of four nonterminal symbols needed to carry out a copying process. The rules generate initially a string of A's and B's, each of which is then replicated and carried to the right end of the string by the copying device. This is a much more interesting result, since it shows that an arbitrary string of symbols can be replicated by a set of rules meeting Restriction 1.) As the reader can verify, this grammar will generate all and only the strings of the desired shape. As we saw in Chapter 3 and in the previous lemma, the effect of Rule 4 can be achieved by an equivalent series of CS rules. Thus the language is a CS language.

To prove the theorem that there are CS languages that are not CF languages, it is next shown that no CF grammar can generate the language just given. This theorem may appear obvious from the fact that the essential step of Rule 4 is not possible without CS rules. But this is precisely what it is necessary to prove in an explicit way.

We may outline a proof as follows (again I depart slightly from Chomsky's formulation). Suppose there is a context-free grammar for the (infinite) language given, with the (necessarily finite by Axiom 4) nonterminal vocabulary $A_1, A_2, \cdots, A_n$. Of these A_i (i.e., the symbols A_1, and so on) there must be some which can dominate an infinite number of different terminal strings (i.e., x's such that $A_i \Rightarrow x$). Eliminate all nonterminal symbols A_j that cannot dominate an infinite number of different strings by replacing all (finitely many) rules $A_i \rightarrow xA_jy$ and $A_j \rightarrow z$ by $A_i \rightarrow xzy$. For every nonterminal symbol A_i it will now be true that there are infinitely many different strings x such that $A_i \Rightarrow x$. Now there must be a nonterminal symbol A_k which appears in the next-to-last line of infinitely many derivations of sentences in the language. This follows from the fact that there is a finite number of symbols in the grammar but an infinity of strings in the language. If all the nonterminal symbols could appear in the next-to-last line of only a finite number of derivations, then there would be only a finite number of sentences (since the product of two finite numbers is also finite). For such a nonterminal symbol, A_k, derive a sentence $\# a^n b^m a^n b^m \#$ where both n and m are greater than r, and r is the length of the longest string of terminal symbols z such that $A_k \rightarrow z$. Every sentence in the language by definition must consist of two separate strings of the same number of a's and two separate strings of the same number of b's. But since from every nonterminal symbol (and hence A_k) an infinity of strings is derivable, we can continue the derivation from the next-to-last line $\# xA_ky \#$ in an infinity of ways to yield an infinity of strings not in the language. Hence the assumed context-free grammar is not a grammar of the language. In other words, the next-to-last line must contain at least one noninterrupted string of n a's and one noninterrupted string of m b's with the end of the string determinable in both cases (since $n, m > r$). Hence, the string which must replace A_k is completely determined by the context in which it appears. But by hypothesis context-restricted rules are not permitted.

The reasons why CF grammars cannot generate languages like the one given are clear enough. For a grammar with a finite set of symbols to generate an infinite set of strings, there must be recursive symbols. In the language described there are four substrings, each of which can assume any finite length. But in every terminal string they are paired off in terms of a simple numerical relationship between the first and the third, the second and the fourth substrings. There are only a limited number of ways of preserving such a relationship (which need not be a relationship of equality as here). One way is to change two recursive elements simultaneously in a single rule. But this would violate all three restrictions. Another possibility is to produce one string and then produce the other by a process of replication through context-sensitive rules. But this is ruled out also for CF grammars. A third possibility is to produce the first pair of numerically related strings by a recursive series of rules, and then introduce a second recursive element between the first pair (and so on). But it is easy to see that this technique can produce only what might be called "nested" languages, that is, those in which the outermost pair of substrings stands in some determinate relationship, as does the next pair toward the center, and so on. In the CS grammar for our language given above, the pairs of equal strings are produced by recursive elements standing next to each other. We might also have described the language as follows:

1. $S \rightarrow a \begin{Bmatrix} S \\ Z \end{Bmatrix} A$
2. $Z \rightarrow b(Z)B$
3. $BA \rightarrow AB$
4. $B \rightarrow b$
5. $A \rightarrow a$

But in either case it is necessary to rearrange strings by CS rules. There remains the possibility of specifying some necessary ordering among the rules, as might be done in a computer program for a grammar of the language. For example, the specification might be: after applying a certain rule skip over certain other rules, so that there are several different routes through the rules. But this ordering reduces to a Type 0 grammar, since the rules must contain addresses telling where to go for the next step, and these addresses are equivalent to nonterminal symbols which are changed at each step along with some other change in the developing string.

The final comparison is between grammars meeting Restriction 2 and those meeting Restriction 3. First it is shown that the Type 3 grammars are essentially finite-state grammars. A finite-state (FS) grammar is a set of triples (x, y, z), where x and z are connected internal states and y is a symbol emitted as the device passes from state x to state z. A finite-state grammar may be represented by a so-called state diagram, that is, a graph with nodes standing for states (including one initial state and one final state) and directed lines connecting various nodes, each line labeled with the symbol emitted at the given transition. For instance, a state diagram for the FS grammar generating the language aa, aba, $abba$, $abbba$, and so on, would be set up as follows (with A both initial and final):

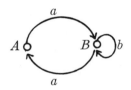

In terms of Turing machines, an FS grammar is a set of quadruples of which the third item is a symbol to be printed onto a blank space (when the second item is the "blank" symbol) or R (except that Turing machines have no alternative choices). It is important to remember that although the number of states is finite, the language generated need not be finite (there may be loops as above).

Restriction 3 limits all rules to the form $A \rightarrow aB$ or $A \rightarrow a$ (where A, B are nonterminal, a is terminal). All that is necessary to show that such a system is essentially the same as an FS grammar is to interpret the nonterminal symbols as designations of

states and to restate the second type of rule as a rule of the form
$A \rightarrow aF$ (where F is a final state with its only transition to the
initial state by a route with $\#$ as the emitted symbol).

Here again, to show that there are languages that can be generated by CF grammars but not by FS grammars, Chomsky refers
to results reported elsewhere (see Chomsky, 1956, and the informal
discussion in Chapter 3 of Chomsky, 1957). Three examples of
non-FS languages are given by Chomsky, of which two (those of
Problem 7, Chapter 2 in this text) are CF languages. (The third,
the language of Problem 5, Chapter 3, is a CS language but not a
CF language.) I shall forego a detailed paraphrase of the proof.
It depends on the fact that languages like the two given consist of
strings with nested dependencies up to any desired number, while
FS grammars pass from state to state with no regard for the route
by which they have arrived at a given state. For instance, in a
string of the "mirror-image" language *aa, bb, abba, baab, aabbaa,*
and so on, the terminal symbol that must be emitted in going from
the next-to-last state to the last depends on which step was taken
on the first transition. The proper transition for the next previous
symbol depends on the second transition, and so on. This means
that for each new string in the language we must construct new
states giving the proper routes leading up to the last (next-to-last,
and so on) transition. But the number of such dependencies is not
limited, whereas there are only a finite number of states in the
grammar.

The final section of the paper gives a long and detailed proof
(compare the later note in Chomsky, 1959b) that it is the property
of self-embedding which distinguishes CF grammars from FS
grammars. A grammar is **self-embedding** if there is a nonterminal
symbol A in its vocabulary such that $A \Rightarrow xAy$ with neither x
nor y null. The proof consists in showing that for every CF grammar that is not self-embedding there is an equivalent FS grammar.
But an FS grammar is not self-embedding, since all of the lines of
its derivations are of the form xB (with B the only nonterminal
symbol in the line). In an FS grammar the rules are either all of
the form $A \rightarrow aB$ or all of the form $A \rightarrow Ba$. (In the latter case

strings will be generated from right to left, but in either case all the lines of the grammar's derivations will have the nonterminal symbol at one end or the other.)

Results of the sort which have been illustrated here are important for several reasons. First, they are steps in the direction of a general theory of linguistic structure in which it will be possible to formulate hypotheses about the classes of systems within which natural languages may be found. Second, if it can be shown that various models are increasingly powerful and that languages beyond the scope of the less powerful ones possess certain structural properties that are shared by natural languages, then we have the strongest kind of evidence that our grammars for natural languages must also transcend the limitations of these simpler models. Convincing demonstrations of this sort have been made to show the inadequacy of finite-state grammars for natural languages, which typically include subparts with indefinite possibilities for self-embedding (see Chomsky, 1956 and 1957); and of context-free phrase-structure grammars (see Postal, 1964). In the latter case, a construction in Mohawk (object incorporation) has been shown to possess the essential property of languages of the form XX where X is a string in a's and b's. English also contains such a subpart in its comparative constructions (see Postal, 1964).

In evaluating such results it is sometimes forgotten that the assumption of recursive processes is necessary for simple and natural descriptions (recall the discussion of the infinitude of sentences in Section 2.1). Thus, suppose we assume that the "mirror-image" language aa, $abba$, $aaaa$, and so on, has an upper limit of length 20 in its terminal strings. The language will now be a finite-state language, but its grammar will be ridiculously complicated and the simplest grammar will probably be a listing of the 2046 different grammatical strings. On the other hand if we allow indefinite recursion we can describe the infinite language with a CF grammar consisting of seven symbols and one rule. But this is, in terms of natural languages, an inconceivably simple language (with two morphemes). Similarly, Postal estimates that although the Mohawk construction could be described by a CS grammar with permutational rules, it would require (with certain minimal assumptions about the size of the relevant vocabulary) something like six million rules to do so! Finally, when we consider not just weak generative power (the ability to enumerate a set of strings) but strong generative power (the ability to assign to the strings a correct structural description), none of the types of grammars considered above are adequate. Thus, recall that it is the power to bring about permutations which gives the CS grammars more generative capacity. But from the point of view of constructing grammars for real languages this is a defect (Section 3.2), since the permutational rules assign the wrong structural descriptions to the generated strings.

In general, the formal study of grammars has shown a good deal about the (weak) generative capacity of grammars that are known to be inadequate for describing natural languages in an empirically satisfying way. On the other hand, a good deal has been learned about applying a more powerful model (transformational grammar) to the description of actual languages, a model which overcomes many of the formal and empirical defects of the phrase-structure grammars. Further research must move along both lines. The mathematical properties of transformational (and possibly other) types of grammars must be studied and the systems tested in the description of more languages. A good deal of careful formulation must be done before comparisons of the sort we have shown in this section can be undertaken. (The reader who wishes to pursue these more abstract questions would do well to read next Chomsky, 1961a; then Chomsky and Miller, 1963; and Chomsky, 1963; both of the latter have very full bibliographies.)

Problems for Chapter 7

1. Write two sets of rules for the following English sentences, one in which the sets of terminal items are disjoint (in which the homonyms must be put into special classes), and one in which there is overlapping.

ay siy bil	hiy wil ček điy ay
ay siy đə siy	fred mey siy mey
hiy siyz wil	bil wil ay đə ček
mey siyz ə ber	đə ber siyz wil

ay mey siy ə ber
mey kænt ber bil
ay wil bil fred
ay wil ček də wil

fred hits də ber
wil wil hit bil
etc.

2. State the relations involved in the following statements, indicate their domains and ranges, and classify them according to transitivity, reflexivity, symmetry, and connexity.

a) English is related to German.
b) The Romance languages are descendents of Latin.
c) English is more closely related to German than to Hindi.
d) English is not related to Ainu.
e) *Green* is an adjective.
f) This sentence consists of a noun phrase and a verb phrase.
g) The sound [p] contrasts with [b].
h) The word *pa*N means 'bread.'
i) The forms x and y are allomorphs of the same morpheme.
j) The phones x and y are allophones of the same phoneme.
k) The sequences x and y are immediate constituents of the same construction.
l) The sequence x is part of a noun phrase (in a given sentence).
m) The sentence S_1 is more grammatical than S_2.
n) The sentence S_1 is not less grammatical than S_2.

3. Show that every relation which is transitive and symmetric is also reflexive.

4. Show that in a system of concatenation there is only one identity element I such that $x + I = I + x = x$.

5. For each of the following languages determine whether it is a CS, CF, or FS language. Draw state diagrams for some of the FS languages. Write grammars for all CS and CF languages. Unless otherwise restricted, assume that n, m, i, j, and so on, are greater than or equal to one ($\geqslant 1$); unless otherwise specified they can equal each other.

a) $a^n b^m c^i$
b) $a^n b^m a^m b^n$
c) $a^n b^m b^i a^j$
d) $b^n a c^m b a^i c$ $(n, m, i \geqslant 0)$
e) $a^n b^m b^i a^j$ $(j \geqslant n, i \geqslant m)$
f) $a^n b^m b^i a^j$ $(j \geqslant m, i \geqslant n)$
g) $a^n b^m a^i b^j$ $(n \leqslant j \leqslant 2n, m \leqslant i \leqslant 3m)$
h) $a^n b^m a^n$
i) $a^n b^m a^n$ $(0 < n \leqslant 5{,}000)$
j) $a^n b^n c^n$
k) $a^n b^{2n} c^{3n}$
l) $a^n b^{n^2} c$ (i.e., abc, $aabbbbc$, $a^3 b^9 c$, $a^4 b^{16} c$, $\cdots$)
m) $a^n b^{n^2}$
n) $a^n b^m$ $(n \neq m)$

CHAPTER EIGHT

PROBLEMS AND PROSPECTS

8.1 Branches of Linguistic Research

The program of linguistic research initiated by the founders of transformational theory is still only in its beginnings. There is no lack of problems yet to be solved or of promising directions for further study, partly in areas that lie beyond the central concerns of linguistic theory. In this our final chapter, a few of these remaining problems and directions will be considered.

In the view followed here, (synchronic) linguistic research (insofar as the formal side of language is concerned) may be divided into the following parts: (a) the formal theory of grammars, that is, the kind of mathematical study outlined and illustrated in the previous chapter; (b) the general theory of language; (c) the use (and testing) of this general theory in constructing theories about particular languages. To these might be added: (d) a study of language use, e.g., theories about the speaker and hearer, and (e) various other studies relating linguistics to other disciplines, as for example psychology (insofar as this does not already fall under (d)), sociology, literary theory, and so on.

Of these various branches only the first is truly independent of empirical testing, and even here there will presumably be a considerable amount of "feedback" from the other parts of linguistic research. The types of languages and grammars that are studied in the abstract will be determined at least in part by the types of rules and distinctions that are needed in actual language description. The interest (beyond the purely mathematical) of comparisons like those made in the preceding chapter stems largely from their implications for the construction of grammars. Indeed, the history of transformational theory mirrors the interactions between the various branches mentioned above. The notion of a grammatical transformation grew originally out of work by Zellig Harris on "discourse analysis" (Harris, 1952a, 1952b), that is, the study of the structure of texts (falling under (d) above). In this work various inadequacies in linguistic theory were uncovered. The attempt to overcome these inadequacies led to a re-examination of general linguistic theory and this in turn to increased attention to the abstract systems underlying various approaches to language description. Finally, the new ideas have led to many new insights (or the recovering of old ones in a new precise form) into the grammatical structure of particular languages. (For Harris's transformations, which are somewhat different from those presented here, see Harris, 1957.)

8.2   The Formal Theory of Grammars

It can be shown convincingly that the description of natural languages is considerably simplified by the addition of a transformational component. It can be shown further that various important relations between sentences and types of constructions can be adequately explained only by transformational rules. One may ask whether there are any stronger reasons for adding a level of transformational rules to a grammar; that is, is it in principle impossible to write a grammar for a natural language (or some natural language) without a transformational component? It can be demonstrated that finite-state grammars and context-free phrase-structure grammars are essentially inadequate to describe a language like English. Can we show in the same way that a context-sensitive phrase-structure grammar is too restricted to generate all and only the sentences of some language? This question has not yet been answered.

A necessary prerequisite to such a demonstration (which involves empirical statements about some real language) is a study of the sort outlined in the last chapter comparing the mathematical properties of transformational grammars and phrase-structure grammars. A negative result would follow from a proof that for every transformational grammar there exists an equivalent phrase-structure grammar (or perhaps phrase-structure plus phonological grammar). Such a proof would, of course, still say nothing about the strong generative capacity of the two types of grammars (recall the discussion at the end of Chapter 7). In terms of the structural descriptions that are provided by a grammar, the evidence seems to be overwhelming that something beyond the apparatus of a PS grammar is necessary.

Short of such a demonstration or in the event of a negative result, many problems remain in characterizing more precisely the relations between sentences that can be described by transformational rules. As an example let us consider the following language (based on Curry, 1961). In this language all the sentences are of the form $\# ab^n cab^m \#$ $(n, m \geq 0)$, and all the *true* sentences are of the form $\# ab^n cab^n \#$, where we may interpret a as 1, xb as "the successor of x" (i.e., a is 1, ab is 2, abb is 3, and so on), and c as "equals." The language is then a language in which we can make such statements as "1 equals 1," "2 equals 2" $(abcab)$, "2 equals 3," and so on. All and only the sentences of the language can be generated by these rules:

1. $S \rightarrow aS_1$

2. $S_1 \rightarrow \begin{Bmatrix} bS_1 \\ S_1 b \\ ca \end{Bmatrix}$

giving *# abbbca #*, *# abcab #*, *# abbbbcabb #*, and so on. Further, all and only the true sentences can be likewise generated by PS rules:

1a. $S \rightarrow T$

3. $T \rightarrow aT_1$

4. $T_1 \rightarrow \begin{Bmatrix} bT_1b \\ ca \end{Bmatrix}$

Now every sentence which is a *T* is a true sentence, but there will be true sentences which are not derived from *T*. Suppose we wish to state certain relations between sentences, such as "equals added to equals are equal," or "equals added to unequals are unequal." This can be done only by a transformational rule. A transformational grammar for this language might take the following form (with *# N #* for 'number' as the initial string):

F 1. $N \rightarrow \begin{Bmatrix} N \\ a \end{Bmatrix} b$

T 1. Optional, false equations
$\begin{rcases} \# \, N \, \# \\ \# \, N' \, \# \end{rcases} \rightarrow \# \, N\mathcal{c}N' \, \#$
Condition: $N \neq N'$

T 2. Obligatory, true equations
$\# \, N \, \# \rightarrow \# \, NcN \, \#$

T 3. Optional, addition of equals
$\begin{rcases} \# \, NcN \, \# \\ \# \, N'cN' \, \# \end{rcases} \rightarrow \# \, NN'cNN' \, \#$

M 1. (obligatory morphophonemic rule)
$bab \rightarrow bbb$

M 2.
$\mathcal{c} \rightarrow c$

It is clear that this grammar is equivalent to the previous one in the sense that it generates the same language. But in terms of the structural information that it gives, it is not equivalent. Besides the possibility of stating general relationships such as those of T 3, we have in this grammar a precise representation of the recursive definition of a number (N): a is a number, and the successor of every number is a number. On the other hand, the PS grammar above provides a strange analysis of the parts of an equation:

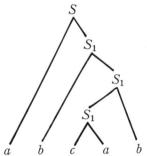

In Chapter 2 we began with a conception of a grammar as a theory or device for generating all of the well-formed or grammatical sentences of a language and none of the ungrammatical ones. Throughout the subsequent chapters we have been developing a more adequate view. We require that a grammar not only generate a set of strings, but also assign to each such string a structural description. The theory of phrase structure presented here is designed to provide just such a description by means of phrase markers. A general problem still to be solved completely is the question of assigning P markers to the strings that have undergone transformational changes. We have discussed this question at some length in Section 4.4. A further question is that of specifying a T marker for each string (see Chomsky, 1955a and 1955b).

The mathematical study of grammars is still only in its beginnings. Transformational theory has leaned heavily on the theory of recursive functions. Other approaches have been made (e.g., by Lambek, 1961, and earlier), and undoubtedly there will be more. With each such new approach there arises the primarily mathematical question of comparing the various models, of restating one theory in the framework of the other, or restating both in terms of some more comprehensive set of concepts.

8.3   The General Theory of Language

A grammar for a specific language forms the basis for a series of predictions of the following sort: If T is a terminal string in phonetic transcription derivable from a grammar G of a language L, then T is in L. That is, the grammar generates only sentences of the language and no nonsentences. Further, if T' is in L, then T' is derivable from G; i.e., all the sentences of the language are derivable from the grammar. Finally, the grammar must assign a set of markers (structural descriptions) to each generated string. The markers form the basis for other predictions about relations between sentences, ambiguity, and so on. In the following section we shall consider the difficult problem of validating grammars, that is, of testing such predictions. Here we shall outline the contribution of a general theory to such predictions.

First of all, the general theory must provide a description of the types of devices or systems from which the grammars of particular languages will be chosen. Most of this book has been concerned with building up a preliminary picture of such systems. That is, the general theory must define such notions as *rule, derivation, transformation*, and so on. Insofar as such notions are usable in describing actual languages, they become part of a general theory of language structure.

Second, aside from specifying the form of grammars, the general theory must provide eventually a set of terms for filling in the substance of the sets of rules, at least in part. This requirement is met, as we have seen, for one part of linguistic theory by a general theory of phonetics, i.e., a set of interpreted symbols to use in the terminal representations T, T', and so forth, mentioned above.

Far more problematical is the question of a general theory of syntactic types or "parts of speech." For many centuries linguistic understanding was dominated by various "universal" theories. It was expected that all languages would conform to a preconceived picture of language structure based on an inadequate logic, a confusion between logic and linguistics, and a set of categories derived through Latin from the Greek grammarians. Such misconceptions (usually combined with a normative approach to language study) are not dead by any means. The reaction to such views was a decision to describe each language in terms of its own structure only and a deep-seated suspicion of any generalizations about linguistic categories of various kinds. But the only thing wrong with the various universal grammars of past times was that they were inadequate, and there is no reason why it should not be possible to construct a general theory of linguistic structure which is "postconceived," that is, based on the study of a wide variety of languages. In order to qualify as a genuine theory — that is, a set of statements from which it is possible to derive predictions that are testable — such a theory must contain universal statements, i.e., hypotheses of the form "for any language L, such and such is true of L."

Such a theory may depend ultimately on a theory of meaning, or its adequacy may be judged according to how well it fits into a broader theory of language that includes a theory of meaning and a theory of language use. Thus, a theory of syntax might provide such general interlingual categories as "individual term," "n-place predicate," "descriptive operator." At the same time the theory might provide general terms for describing how such universal categories are implemented in specific languages: "case," "noun," "prefix," "government." The eventual outcome of such a theory might be a theory of language typology based not on comparisons of texts, but on the comparison of grammars. For instance, purely isolating and purely agglutinative languages would presumably differ from fusional languages by having no rules of the form

$$x + y \rightarrow z.$$

(A recent study of Cantonese grammar contains only two morphophonemic rules, that is, rules in which certain phonemic consequences result from certain morphemic combinations. See Yue, 1963.)

Even if the general theory reaches such a point of development, it will still not be complete without a further part, namely, a method for evaluating grammars. Two grammars for the same language might be equally complete and correct, and we wish our general theory to provide a criterion of choice between them. Of two theories that cover the same facts, it is usual to choose that one which is simpler (or more economical). It seems natural to identify simplicity with the number of symbol tokens (i.e., occurrences of symbols) in the grammar. We would exclude from our count symbols of the metatheory — i.e., concatenation signs, parentheses, arrows, and so on — and count as single symbols whatever appears between these signs, i.e., the primes of the various parts of the grammar. This consideration seems to underlie many statements about "pattern congruity" and the like. For instance, suppose we have a language with three initial aspirated stops (bilabial, alveolar, velar) and three final unaspirated stops. The simplest description of the allophones of the three phonemes we set up will be the one normally chosen on the basis of phonetic similarity, parallel distribution of allophones, and so on. That is, if we set up /P/, /T/, /K/ with /P/ an aspirated bilabial stop initially but an unaspirated alveolar stop finally, and so forth, our description will use more symbols for articulations than will the natural description.

There are several difficulties connected with the notion of simplicity. Before discussing them, however, it would be well to clear away several misconceptions. First of all, this criterion does not provide a useful means for discovering when we have *the* simplest grammar possible (to expect this would be somewhat like asking for a criterion of absolute truth). Second, it has never happened that there have been two equally complete and correct grammars for the same language. The inclusion of this notion in a general theory of language does not mean that the investigator must write two grammars for every language he studies and then apply the measure of simplicity. Rather, linguistic investigation takes place like any other kind of scientific activity. A linguist provides a description of a language which is as good as he can make it in a limited time and with limited knowledge and abilities (i.e., a human product). At each step he thinks of numerous alternatives, and he rejects many when he sees that they will lead to blind alleys or when he recognizes connections between seemingly disparate facts that can be accounted for by a more general statement. Occasionally, he will carry out two alternative partial analyses in considerable detail before choosing between them. Accepting the criterion of simplicity merely means that he makes his choices not on the basis of some a priori notion about language structure — that constructions must be binary, that there must be no zero elements, or such principles as "once a phoneme always a phoneme" — but only on the basis of the economy of the whole description. Sooner or later his work will be superseded. Generally, since grammatical theories like other theories are never complete, a new theory will not be merely simpler than the one it is intended to replace. It will account for new facts as well or will be more correct in the sense that it excludes certain nonsentences generated by the other theory, or explains better certain connections between sentences, and so on.

The criterion of simplicity seems to work well within each component of a grammar. It seems to be supported by other judgments in terms of general notions of linguistic form and explanatory power. For instance, we surely would prefer a theory with a single general statement applying to a large class of items to one generating the same combinations by means of a large number of special statements. Similarly, if the rules can be set up in such a way that the number of statements which refer to special environments is minimized, such an analysis will be preferred. But both of these choices are supported by the criterion of simplicity (see Halle, 1961 and 1962). On the other hand, when there is a question of choosing between two analyses that cut across from one part of a grammar to another, the situation is not so clear. In the discussion of a segment of Japanese grammar in Chapter 5 some of the considerations entering into such decisions were illustrated. Ultimately, we must try out various alternatives in weighting symbols for various parts of a grammar and examine their consequences (for some discussion of this point, see Chomsky, 1955b, Chapter 9).

It is important to remember that "simplicity" is being used here as a technical term to be defined in general linguistic theory, and that various possible definitions for "simplicity" must be examined as to their empirical consequences (just as the terms of a general theory of phonology must be so tested). The inclusion of such a term in general linguistic theory — along with such terms as *rule, derivation, transformation* — results from the attempt to provide an evaluation procedure in the general theory. If the results of using this term in a certain way (e.g., by counting symbols) lead to predictions that jibe with various facts about languages and their use, then the term (like other hypothetical terms of the general theory) can be taken to indicate a significant feature of languages in general. Thus, consider another possible measure of simplicity as being not the number of occurrences of symbols in the rules of a grammar (number of tokens) but the number of primes (types) set up in the theory. But this supposition leads to the absurd result that all languages have the same number of primes (namely, two) on the various levels (e.g., phonemics), since any set of rules can be coded into a binary system. Or consider the proposal that simplicity be measured by the number of rules. Here again we can achieve trivial simplifications merely by taking large sets of rules (in fact, the whole set of PS rules, for instance) and making one rule (with square brackets) out of them. On the other hand, counting occurrences of symbols leads to significant simplifications in the sense that the use of abbreviative devices will mirror many of those general statements that would be made in a less formal and more intuitive presentation of the system of a language.

This discussion becomes meaningful only against the background of linguistic thought as it has developed in the last three or four decades. The discussion of the foundations of linguistic theory has been carried on with a strong admixture of the philosophy of science (and occasionally metaphysics). Linguistics followed a trend in the philosophy of science and in methodological discussion (especially in the social sciences) which reached its peak in the late twenties and early thirties. In line with this trend, linguistics attempted to frame its basic concepts in operational terms (with a strong Baconian slant). Much discussion was devoted to various justifications for analyses of linguistic systems in terms of various procedures to be followed (or which might in principle be followed if one wanted to guarantee "rigorous" results). Stated most crudely, the hope seemed to be that a series of mechanical procedures (an algorithm) could be stated which would automatically lead to a correct linguistic description. It is doubtful whether many linguists would have subscribed to this notion in such a bald form, but an examination of the literature of the forties and early fifties cannot fail to show that this idea underlay much of the thinking of the time.

The point of view followed here puts forward a much weaker claim, namely, that it is possible to construct a general theory which will provide a significant method for choosing between two grammatical theories. One may ask whether this is not also too much to hope for from a scientific theory — after all, no other science can make such a claim. But it must be remembered that we are dealing in linguistics with relatively simple systems (compared say to biological or physical systems), which are learned by normal humans in a few years without conscious teaching on the part of the community (although no one who has watched a child learn a language can say that it takes place without effort). Ultimately, we may hope to learn something about how this relatively rapid learning takes place. But the prior problem is a specification of the types of systems from which grammars are chosen. (Much of the literature has been concerned with discussing these various "goals of linguistic theory." See, e.g., Chomsky, 1957, 1962c.)

8.4 Empirical Tests

In the last section we mentioned a few of the predictions that can be made on the basis of a given grammar for a language. Clearly, if linguistics is not to be a branch of metaphysics, it must be possible to test such predictions (and others of a different sort).

But testing predictions in a science which deals with a cultural institution is by no means a simple matter.

Suppose that we have a grammar G for a language L, and suppose further that we have some means for synthesizing utterances from the G terminal strings (e.g., by an electronic device like a Vocoder, or by pronunciation rules for a phonetic virtuoso who does not know the language). Testing the grammar involves several steps: (1) deriving G terminal strings, (2) discovering whether a particular string is in L, (3) finding and transcribing sentences of L directly, (4) testing to see whether these transcribed sentences of L are derivable from G. The first two processes are concerned with discovering whether G describes only sentences of L; the latter two are concerned with discovering whether G describes all the sentences of L. At each point there are numerous traps and difficulties.

First of all, we must take care that we do not unwittingly make our grammar appear more refined than it actually is by choosing only the reasonable sentences that can be derived from it and neglecting many nonsentences that might also be derivable. For instance, in a grammar of English in which *man, boy, ball, magic,* and *sentence* are all lumped into one terminal class, we will be able to derive all sorts of reasonable sentences: *The man hit the boy, A boy threw a ball, The man derived the sentence, The boy was afraid of magic.* But the grammar will also generate *A ball threw the boy, The sentence was afraid of boy, The man derived a magic.* To ensure that it is the grammar alone that is providing the description, it is often helpful to produce random derivations by someone with no knowledge of the language being described. As grammatical descriptions grow more complex and detailed, it is to be hoped that checking the theories may be made easier by programming a computer to carry out such random derivations.

The second step given above involves the difficult matter of finding some experimental test for grammaticality. One obvious test would be to ask for each string derivable from the grammar "Is this sentence in L?" (i.e., we ask an informant "Can you say such and such?"). This is probably the most frequent type of test in any kind of linguistic description (including the case where the linguist is his own informant). There are difficulties in such a procedure. People are notoriously inconsistent in what they think they say (or should say) and what they actually say. If we were working with a certain kind of English informant, he might reject *It's me*, even if he regularly used this sentence. Other tests have been suggested. Thus, we might have informants read sentences and compare their renditions for grammatical and ungrammatical strings (as predicted by some grammar) on the assumption that the renditions of ungrammatical sequences will be marked by more hesitations, by the intonations that are used for giving lists of unconnected items, and so on. Or we might test the retentions of grammatical and ungrammatical strings on the theory that informants will be able to remember and reproduce grammatical sequences better than ungrammatical ones of the same length. Thus, there is one sequence that I have used repeatedly in classes to illustrate the restrictions on attaching relative clauses in English: *I see the cat that the mat that is on is dirty.* I can never remember the form of this ungrammatical sequence from one occasion to the next, but am forced to work it out each time with pencil and paper.

In this discussion we have assumed that the set of all sequences of the elements of a grammar is partitioned into two subsets only, the grammatical sequences and the ungrammatical ones. Instead of this essentially classificatory concept, it is possible to work with a more refined comparative concept (on classificatory, comparative, and quantitative concepts, see Carnap, 1950). That is, we consider a scheme that will lead to such predictions as "S_1 is more grammatical than (or perhaps is not less grammatical than) S_2." This notion is more satisfactory than a simple dichotomy for several reasons. We are often hard put to it to make an absolute decision as to whether a given sentence is or is not grammatical. But we will more willingly compare two sentences as to grammaticality. For instance, *Who is that fly you were talking to?* may or may not be considered grammatical by a particular judge. But it would probably be judged by most subjects as more grammatical than

Who is that you fly were to talking? and less grammatical than
Who is that girl you were talking to?

A comparative concept of grammaticality also makes possible
more refined testing. Consider the following situation. Suppose we
predict that four sequences of terminal items will be ranked in a
given order of increasing grammaticality. We ask informants to
rank the sentences according to some such criterion (perhaps by
approximation to "ordinary English" or the like). There are 4! = 24
possible ways of ranking the sentences, so that a subject with no
knowledge whatsoever of English would have one chance out of
twenty-four of guessing the predicted order. If, on the other hand,
we ask the subjects simply to class the sentences into grammatical
or ungrammatical, there will be 2^4 (16) possible classifications so
that a subject with no knowledge of the language has a one-
sixteenth chance of making the predicted assignment. Clearly,
agreement on the ranking of the sentences will be more significant
than will agreement on classification according to a dichotomous
scale. Even if we ask the subjects to classify into two types, we
can still use the comparative concept to predict an arrangement
of the sentences into a series ranging from the one which most
subjects agreed was grammatical to the one which fewest subjects
agreed was grammatical. (On such problems see Hill, 1961; Maclay
and Sleator, 1960; Chomsky, 1961b.)

Besides questions of grammaticality, there are other areas in
which to test the correctness of a grammatical theory. Thus, we
have already considered the importance of predicting ambiguity
(an empirical concept) whenever there is constructional homonymity (a structural concept). In this area as well as in the question
of judging grammaticality, it is important to take into account the
significance of (linguistic and nonlinguistic) context: many ambiguities are never noticed because the various possible meanings are
narrowed down by context. The native speaker's judgments about
the structural relations between sets of sentences may also be used
to validate grammatical theories. For instance, we ask if he will
classify *Who is coming?* and *Is he coming?* as instances of one type
of sentence as against *John is coming.* (This was the case with a

six-year-old naïve expert speaker of English.) Here it will often be
the case that the judgments of the native speaker are colored by
the correct or incorrect grammar of the classroom. Generally
speaking, it seems that unsophisticated speakers are more predictable than highly educated ones (thus, the author has found the
same six-year-old informant unerring in her judgments of such
examples of ungrammatical sentences as *Read you a book on modern
music?*, *The child seems sleeping*, and other sentences about colorless
ideas, green horses, and oranges).

Before leaving the question of validating theories (which is in
need of much more study), we must mention the other two steps
given above. What we have discussed so far is relevant to deciding
whether a grammar describes only grammatical sentences. To find
sequences derivable from a grammar and to show that they are
not in the language being described will indicate that the grammar
is defective. Finding new sentences and showing that they are not
derivable does not prove that the grammar is incorrect but only
that it is incomplete. Such searching is clearly important if we are
to have adequate grammatical theories. One application of linguistic theory that can play a role in testing the completeness of
grammars is machine translation, although this field involves not
just grammatical theory but the study of the use of grammatical
theories by devices of finite capacity and a specific structure.
(Most of the critiques of transformational analyses that have
appeared have not concerned themselves with showing that published rules generate ungrammatical sequences, but rather with
giving examples of sentences that cannot be handled by the rules.
See e.g. Bolinger, 1961.)

8.5   Conclusions

There are many other problems that might be discussed here, and
there are some that have been touched on throughout the course
of this introduction (for instance, the ordering of transformational
rules, Section 4.4). Only time will tell whether the suggestions for
a general theory of linguistic structure made in transformational

theory will be adequate. But if the success of a new theory is to be judged partly by the issues it has raised and the re-examination of basic assumptions that it has stimulated, then it would seem that transformational theory has been very successful indeed. I shall close with a mention of some of the basic theses that have been raised in recent discussion (and are still being argued).

A sharp distinction must be drawn between the heuristic procedures ("discovery procedures") by which one arrives at a theory and the validation of the theory itself. Whether one arrives at a hypothesis by sifting vast amounts of material or whether it pops into one's head while shaving is irrelevant. What is relevant is how well the hypothesis fits into an integrated description and whether the integrated description is correct and complete.

A grammar must be a predictive theory which will project an unlimited number of new sentences not in the original corpus. This view brings with it two corollaries. General linguistic theory must provide a precise characterization of the way in which a theory can be said to "predict" a given sentence. There must be some recursive devices or rules in a grammatical description. Further, a grammar must assign a structural description to each sentence that it enumerates. Again, the way in which this assignment takes place must be precisely specified by the general theory.

A grammatical theory is not a direct model of the user of a language (either speaker or hearer). We have not discussed the interesting question of just how a language is put to use by a device with certain capacities and a finite memory. There has been a good deal of discussion recently of the limitations on certain kinds of "depth" in natural languages. Most of these discussions have failed to make the distinction between the two types of questions. (See Yngve, 1960, 1961; see also the critiques in Chomsky, 1961a; and in Miller and Chomsky, 1963.) In order not to prejudge our theories of the use of language, however, linguistic theory should proceed without assuming anything about the structure of the human brain. Given a theory of a language, we can then proceed to certain hypotheses about its use. For instance, we can predict that certain self-embedding structures will not exceed a certain limit and that there will be significant differences between spoken styles and written styles (where the innate limitations are overcome by pencil and paper).

Finally, there is a good deal of empirical evidence that can be brought to bear on evaluating the adequacy of a grammar beyond the simple fact (!) that such and such an utterance occurred. Such evidence has to do with what is described vaguely enough by such terms as "linguistic intuition," or "relations between sentences," and often even "meaning."

In his book on *The Logic of the Sciences and the Humanities* (1947), F. S. C. Northrop has argued that there are different stages in the development of any science and that there is hence no universally valid answer to the question: What is scientific method? In particular, he distinguishes between the "natural history" stage, where the primary emphasis is on data gathering and classification, and the deductive stage, in which precise axiomatic theories are constructed. The present situation in American linguistics seems to illustrate beautifully the confrontation (and the clash) between these two stages. Many linguists appear to be impatient with the transformational approach and its insistence on logical niceties and heavy emphasis on "pure syntax" in Carnap's sense (i.e., the study of possible formal properties of grammars and languages). And from the point of view that considers the urgent task of setting down data on the vast number of undescribed languages (many fast disappearing), they are right. On the other hand, transformational theorists become impatient with relatively crude and vague attempts to theorize about language on the basis of a narrowly reductionist philosophy of science. And they, too, are right. We must distinguish sharply between the theories about particular languages and the metatheory about these theories. In a search for a metatheory, in an attempt to reconstruct precisely the "logical structure of linguistic theory," the transformationalists have provided elegant and powerful tools for the description of particular languages. But clearly there is room in the universe of linguistics for both kinds of work. There must be both theory and application; the feedback in both directions is fruitful. As Kant

said, "Ideas without content are empty, intuitions [i.e., obser-
vations] without concepts are blind." It is only by formulating
precise and general hypotheses about language that we can hope
to understand this most universal and characteristic human ac-
complishment. It is only by detailed study of many languages that
we can test and deepen this understanding.

SELECTED BIBLIOGRAPHY

The date given for all published work is the date of publication. In some cases, as in various papers presented at conferences, the sequence of development is more accurately reflected in the date of the conference. I have included a few items which were not referred to explicitly in the text.

Bach, Emmon. 1962a. "The Order of Elements in a Transformational Grammar of German." *Language* 38:263–9.

———. 1962b. "Subcategories in Transformational Grammars." To appear in *Proceedings of the IX International Congress of Linguists*.

Berge, Claude. 1958. *Théorie des graphes et ses applications*. Paris.

Birkhoff, Garrett, and Saunders MacLane. 1953. *A Survey of Modern Algebra*. Revised edition. New York.

Bloomfield, Leonard. 1933. *Language*. New York.

Bolinger, Dwight L. 1961. "Syntactic Blends and other Matters." *Language* 37:366–81.

Carnap, Rudolf. 1939. *Foundations of Logic and Mathematics* (identical with *International Encyclopedia of Unified Science*, Vol. I, No. 3). Chicago.

———. 1950. *Logical Foundations of Probability*. Chicago.

———. 1958. *Introduction to Symbolic Logic and its Applications*, trans. by William H. Meyer and John Wilkinson. New York.

Chomsky, Noam. 1955a. *Transformational Analysis*. Dissertation, University of Pennsylvania. (Essentially Chapter VIII of the following.)

———. [1955b.] *The Logical Structure of Linguistic Theory*. (Dittographed, no date or place. Available on microfilm from the Massachusetts Institute of Technology library.)

———. 1956. "Three Models for the Description of Language." *I. R. E.* [Institute of Radio Engineers] *Transactions on Information Theory*, IT-2, pp. 113–24.

———. 1957. *Syntactic Structures* (identical with *Janua Linguarum*, IV). The Hague. (The second printing, 1962, contains additional bibliography.)

———. 1959a. "On Certain Formal Properties of Grammars." *Information and Control* 2:137–67.

Chomsky, Noam (cont.). 1959b. "A Note on Phrase Structure Grammars." *Information and Control* 2:393–5.

———. 1961a. "On the Notion 'Rule of Grammar'." In Jakobson, 1961, pp. 6–24.

———. 1961b. "Some Methodological Remarks on Generative Grammar." *Word* 17:219–39.

———. 1962a. "A Transformational Approach to Syntax." In Hill, 1962, pp. 124–58 (see also the following discussion, pp. 158 ff.).

———. 1962b. "The Logical Basis of Linguistic Theory." To appear in *Proceedings of the IX International Congress of Linguists*.

———. 1962c. "Explanatory Models in Linguistics." In *Logic, Methodology, and Philosophy of Science: Proceedings of the 1960 International Congress*, pp. 528–50. Eds. Ernest Nagel, Patrick Suppes and Alfred Tarski. Stanford.

———. 1963. "Formal Properties of Grammars." *Handbook of Mathematical Psychology*, II, 323–418. Eds. R. Duncan Luce, Robert R. Bush, and Eugene Galanter. New York and London.

Chomsky, Noam, Morris Halle, and Fred Lukoff. 1956. "On Accent and Juncture in English." *For Roman Jakobson*, pp. 65–80. The Hague.

Chomsky, Noam, and George A. Miller. 1958. "Finite State Languages." *Information and Control* 1:91–112.

———. 1963. "Introduction to the Formal Analysis of Natural Languages." *Handbook of Mathematical Psychology*, II, 269–321. Eds. R. Duncan Luce, Robert R. Bush, and Eugene Galanter. New York and London.

Curry, Haskell B. 1961. "Some Logical Aspects of Grammatical Structure." In Jakobson, 1961, pp. 56–68.

Davis, Martin. 1958. *Computability and Unsolvability*. New York, Toronto, London.

Elson, Benjamin, and Velma B. Pickett. 1962. *An Introduction to Morphology and Syntax*. Santa Ana.

Gleason, H. A., Jr. 1955. *Workbook in Descriptive Linguistics*. New York.

———. 1961. *An Introduction to Descriptive Linguistics*. Revised edition. New York.

Goodstein, R. L. 1957. *Recursive Number Theory*. Amsterdam.

Halle, Morris. 1959. *The Sound Pattern of Russian*. The Hague.

———. 1961. "On the Role of Simplicity in Linguistic Descriptions." In Jakobson, 1961, pp. 89–94.

———. 1962. "Phonology in Generative Grammar." *Word* 18:54–72.

Halle, Morris, and Noam Chomsky. Forthcoming. *The Sound Pattern of English*.

Harms, Robert T. 1962. *Estonian Grammar* (identical with *Indiana University Publications, Uralic and Altaic Series*, Vol. 12). Bloomington, Indiana, and The Hague.

Harris, Zellig S. 1951. *Methods in Structural Linguistics*. Chicago. (Paperbound edition: *Structural Linguistics*.)

———. 1952a. "Discourse Analysis." *Language* 28:1–30.

———. 1952b. "Discourse Analysis: a Sample Text." *Language* 28:474–94.

———. 1957. "Co-occurrence and Transformation in Linguistic Structure." *Language* 33:283–340.

Hempel, Carl G. 1952. *Fundamentals of Concept Formation in Empirical Science* (identical with *International Encyclopedia of Unified Science*, Vol. II, No. 7). Chicago.

Hill, Archibald A. 1958. *Introduction to Linguistic Structures*. New York.

———. 1961. "Grammaticality." *Word* 17:1–10.

———, ed. 1962. *Third Texas Conference on Problems of Linguistic Analysis in English*. Austin. (Conference held in 1958.)

Hockett, Charles F. 1958. *A Course in Modern Linguistics*. New York.

Jakobson, Roman, ed. 1961. *Structure of Language and its Mathematical Aspects* (identical with *Proceedings of Symposia in Applied Mathematics*, Vol. XII). Providence. (Conference held in 1960.)

Jakobson, Roman, and Morris Halle. 1956. *Fundamentals of Language* (identical with *Janua Linguarum*, I). The Hague.

Jakobson, Roman, C. G. M. Fant, and Morris Halle. 1952. *Preliminaries to Speech Analysis* (identical with *M.I.T. Acoustics Laboratory Technical Report* No. 13). Cambridge, Mass.

Joos, Martin, ed. 1958. *Readings in Linguistics*. Second edition. New York.

Kamke, Erich. 1962. *Mengenlehre* (fourth edition). Berlin. (Translation of second edition by F. Bagemihl: *Theory of Sets*, New York, 1950.)

Lambek, Joachim. 1961. "On the Calculus of Syntactic Types." In Jakobson, 1961, pp. 166–78.

Lees, Robert B. 1957. Review of Chomsky, 1957, *Language* 33:375–408.

———. 1960. *The Grammar of English Nominalizations*. *Indiana U. Research Center in Anthropology, Folklore, and Linguistics*, Publication 12 (identical with *IJAL*, XXVI, No. 3, Part II). Bloomington, Indiana.

———. 1961a. "O Pereformulirovanij Transformacionnyx Grammatik" ['On Reformulating Transformational Grammars']. *Voprosy Jazykoznanija*, X, No. 6, pp. 41–50.

———. 1961b. *The Phonology of Modern Standard Turkish* (identical with *Indiana University Publications, Uralic and Altaic Series*, Vol. 6). Bloomington, Indiana, and The Hague.

Lees, Robert B., and E. S. Klima. 1963. "Rules for English Pronominalization." *Language* 39:17–28.

Leopold, Werner F. 1948. "German ch." *Language* 24:179–80. (Reprinted in Joos, 1958, pp. 215 f.)

Longacre, Robert E. 1960. "String Constituent Analysis." *Language* 36:63–88.

Lounsbury, Floyd G. 1953. *Oneida Verb Morphology* (identical with *Yale University Publications in Anthropology*, No. 48). New Haven. (Excerpt reprinted in Joos, 1958, pp. 379–85, as "The Method of Descriptive Morphology.")

Maclay, Howard, and Mary D. Sleator. 1960. "Responses to Language: Judgments of Grammaticalness." *IJAL* 26:275–82.

Merrifield, William R., Constance M. Naish, Calvin R. Rensch, and Gillian Story. 1962. *Laboratory Manual for Morphology and Syntax*. Santa Ana.

Miller, George A., and Noam Chomsky. 1963. "Finitary Models of Language Users." *Handbook of Mathematical Psychology*, II, 419–91. Eds. R. Duncan Luce, Robert R. Bush, and Eugene Galanter. New York and London.

Morris, Charles W. 1938. *Foundations of the Theory of Signs* (identical with *International Encyclopedia of Unified Science*, Vol. I, No. 2). Chicago.

Moulton, William G. 1947. "Juncture in Modern Standard German." *Language* 24:212–26. (Reprinted in Joos, 1958, pp. 208–15.)

Nida, Eugene A. 1949. *Morphology: The Descriptive Analysis of Words*, 2nd ed. Ann Arbor.

Northrop, F. S. C. 1947. *The Logic of the Sciences and the Humanities*. New York.

Peterson, Gordon E., and Frank Harary. 1961. "Foundations of Phonemic Theory." In Jakobson, 1961, pp. 139–65.

Pike, Kenneth L. 1943. *Phonetics*. Ann Arbor.

Plath, Warren. 1961. "Mathematical Linguistics." *Trends in European and American Linguistics: 1930–1960*, pp. 21–57. Eds. Christine Mohrmann, Alf Sommerfelt, and Joshua Whatmough. Utrecht.

Postal, Paul M. 1964. "Some Further Limitations of Phrase Structure Grammars." To appear in *Readings in the Philosophy of Language*. Eds. J. Katz and J. Fodor.

———. Forthcoming. *Constituent Structure: A Study of Contemporary Models of Syntactic Description*. (To appear as a supplement to *IJAL*.)

Putnam, Hilary. 1961. "Some Issues in the Theory of Grammar." In Jakobson, 1961, pp. 25–42.

Quine, Willard Van Orman. 1951. *Mathematical Logic*. Revised edition. Cambridge, Mass.

Rosenbloom, Paul. 1950. *The Elements of Mathematical Logic.* New York.

Saporta, Sol, and Heles Contreras. 1962. *A Phonological Grammar of Spanish.* Seattle.

Schachter, Paul. 1962a. Review of Lees, 1960, *IJAL* 28:134–46.

———. 1962b. "Kernel and Non-kernel Sentences in Transformational Grammar." To appear in *Proceedings of the IX International Congress of Linguists.*

Shannon, C. E., and W. Weaver. 1949. *The Mathematical Theory of Communication.* Urbana.

Smith, Carlota S. 1961. "A Class of Complex Modifiers in English." *Language* 37:343–65.

Smith, Henry Lee, Jr. 1962. "Syntactic Analysis and a General Theory of Levels." In Hill, 1962, pp. 86–107.

Smith, Richard E. 1962. *A Transformational Sketch of Japanese.* Unpublished M. A. Thesis, University of Texas.

Stockwell, Robert P. 1960. "The Place of Intonation in a Generative Grammar of English." *Language* 36:360–7.

Suppes, Patrick C. 1960. *Axiomatic Set Theory.* Princeton.

Wells, Rulon S. 1947. "Immediate Constituents." *Language* 23:81–117. (Reprinted in Joos, 1958, pp. 186–207.)

Yngve, Victor H. 1960. "A Model and an Hypothesis for Language Structure." *Proceedings of the American Philosophical Society*, Vol. 104, No. 5, pp. 444–66.

———. 1961. "The Depth Hypothesis." In Jakobson, 1961, pp. 130–8.

Yue, Anne Oi Kan. 1963. *A Transformational Outline of Cantonese Grammar.* Unpublished M. A. Thesis, University of Texas.

INDEXES

SUBJECT INDEX

INDEX OF SPECIAL SYMBOLS